THE WAR OF LOST OPPORTUNITIES

The War of Lost Opportunities

General Max Hoffmann

The Naval & Military Press Ltd

Published by

The Naval & Military Press Ltd
Unit 10 Ridgewood Industrial Park,
Uckfield, East Sussex,
TN22 5QE England

Tel: +44 (0) 1825 749494
Fax: +44 (0) 1825 765701

www.naval-military-press.com
www.military-genealogy.com
www.militarymaproom.com

CONTENTS

The
War of Lost Opportunities

CHAPTER I

RUSSO-JAPANESE REFLECTIONS

THE order for mobilization found me at Mülhausen in Alsace, where I had been, for a year, the commander of a battalion in Prince Wilhelm's Baden Infantry Regiment. For the last two years my mobilization orders had been : " First General Staff Officer " to the Commander-in-Chief of the detachments appointed for the Eastern Theatre of War. This employment was familiar to me ; I had served as lieutenant and commander of a company, and I had likewise had various other appointments on the General Staff in East Prussia and Posen. Having been stationed in East Prussia during seven years, it had become like a second home to me.

I knew the Russian Army both theoretically and practically. In the winter of 1898-99, after I had passed my examinations at the Staff College, and as Russian interpreter, I had been sent for six months to Russia and afterwards for five years I had been attached to the Russian department of the Great General Staff. Besides this I had also gone through the Russo-Japanese War as military attaché on the Japanese side. I had been with the second Japanese division at the Mo-tien-ling pass near Liauyang, at Shakaho and Mukden, and I had seen the Russians fight.

I wish to remark here that the Russians had unquestionably learned very much in the Japanese War. If in the campaign against us they had acted in the same undecided manner, if they had attacked in the same defective way and if they had reacted in the same nervous manner to every threatened attack from the flank ; if they had thrown away uselessly as many of their reserves, as they did in the Manchurian campaign, the struggle would have been much easier for us.

In every battle, Kuropatkin, the Russian Commander-in-Chief, in the Manchurian campaign, had victory in his hand ; he only required to have the firm resolve of closing his hand in order to grasp the victory, but he never had the energy to take this resolve.

The battle of Liauyang was a typical example of his method. The Japanese frontal attack on Liauyang from the south had miscarried. General Kuroki decided to make the bold attempt of withdrawing the mass of his First Army across the Taitsu-Ho and to bring about a decision by attacking the heights east of Liauyang. Between the Taitsu-Ho and the Division of the Guards that was fighting in connection with the Fourth Japanese Army—a distance of about five English miles—he only left six companies, which were distributed in small groups on the summits of the hills, to deceive the Russians into the belief that they were strongly held. The Russians had only to attack these points for the fate of the Japanese Army to have been sealed. The Division of the Guards would then have been encircled, the First and Second Japanese Armies would have been forced to the south-west, and Kuroki would have been driven into the hills. I myself passed forty-eight hours with one of these Japanese Groups ; we had the Russians, at a distance of 2500-3000 metres in thickly lined trenches in front of us ; they did not move. When Kuroki's troops made themselves felt on the North bank of the Taitsu-Ho, and the 15th Brigade attacked the Knoll, that the Japanese call Manju-Yama, and the Russians Hsi-Kuan-tun, Kuropatkin's whole attention and care was concentrated upon this one point. The whole of his reserves were massed in this one menaced spot and exhausted in hopeless counter-attacks on the Knoll that the 15th Brigade had taken. The Southern front, where an easy success was beckoning to him was taken no account of ; and when it became clear that they could not retake the little Knoll Hsi-Kuan-tun, a retirement was ordered, without any reason. Thus it was at Liauyang and likewise at Strako and Mukden.

This was not the method of war the Russians adopted against us. The mistakes they had made when opposed to the Japanese they did not repeat in the campaign against us.

One of my last tasks while I was in the Russian department of the Great General Staff was to construct the plan of a Russian attack on Germany, from the information we possessed. Our intelligence service had not worked very well during the years of peace. The chief cause of this was, that the large sums of money, that are necessary to enlist agents and spies abroad, were not at its disposal.

As far as I can remember it was only once, in

the year 1902, that we succeeded in buying the whole Russian plan of attack from a colonel in the General Staff. From that time on we only knew, that the plan had been changed, but in what way remained doubtful for many long years. In the year 1910—if I am not mistaken—the Intelligence Officer, Captain Nicolai, of the General Staff of the First Army Corps in Königsberg was able to obtain a copy of orders for the defence of the frontier by a detachment of the 26th Russian Division that was then stationed at Kovno. From this it appeared, that of the troops which would at first be at their disposal, the Russians would advance two Armies against us : the so-called Vilna Army and the Warsaw Army. They were both to attack East Prussia, the one from the North and the other from the South of the Masurian Lakes. The two Armies were to advance their inner wings in the direction of Gerdauen and attempt a junction behind the chain of the Masurian Lakes. The orders we had in our hands gave no instructions about the formation of the two armies. At first the troops belonging to the military district of Warsaw and those belonging to the military district of Vilna were naturally to form part of the force. The troops that were stationed in the Southern portion of the Warsaw district and those stationed in the military districts of Kiev and Odessa were destined for the advance on Austria-Hungary. On the other hand, we knew nothing about the probable employment of the troops in the military districts of Petersburg, Finland, Moscow, Kasan, the Caucasus and all the Asiatic troops. With regard to the last named, our General Staff took it for granted, at least as long as I was in the Russian department (Autumn, 1911), that the Russians would not be in a position to throw them all into Europe, as they supposed that our diplomacy would succeed in keeping Japan from joining the alliance of our enemies. If our Foreign Office succeeded in this, which according to ordinary human understanding seemed no very difficult task, the Russians would be obliged to keep at least part of their East Siberian troops in the Far East.

It is true, I personally could not allay certain apprehensions that I had concerning our relations with Japan. I remember a remark made in the Spring of 1907 by Terautsi, who was then Minister of War. Report said that Terautsi was not very favourably disposed towards us Germans. At a dinner party the conversation turned upon this point. Terautsi admitted that his opinion was formed not so much on account of the German military measures as of German politics, and that Germany, moreover, was to blame for Japan making war on Russia.

" In 1897 we took Port Arthur from the Chinese " Terautsi said, " and we were in possession of it. The Ultimatum of Germany, France and Russia forced us to surrender Port Arthur to the Chinese. That Russia sent us the Ultimatum was comprehensible. They were aspiring to the possession of Port Arthur, and the ice-free port of Dalni. That France supported her was natural as she was allied with France. But what had you to do with the whole matter ? "

I asked myself the same question, more especially when I heard that the Ambassador we had at the time in Tokio had allowed himself, and as far as I know, without any instructions from the Wilhelm-strasse, and in no very skilful manner, to be pushed forward by his more clever colleagues from Paris and Petersburg at the presentation of the Ultimatum.

I remember, when in the winter of 1905, I was standing with my wife in Shimonoseki before the tea-house where the Peace was signed, having given expression to this fear : " Let us hope that some day we shall not have to pay for this stupidity."

Unfortunately, my fears were realized, and the Japanese Ultimatum, which caused such an unwarranted storm of indignation among us Germans, was nothing more than a literal translation of the Ultimatum of the year 1897, only in place of the words " Port Arthur " the word " Tsingtau " had been inserted.

I have just mentioned General Terautsi. In the first campaign he had gone through as a young man, during the Civil War of 1888, he had been wounded in the arm by an arrow. In consequence of this wound his arm remained stiff. He always appeared to me as a symbol of the rapid development of the Japanese army. In the short space of thirty years it had advanced from being armed with bows and arrows to machine guns and modern breech-loading firearms, and the man who in his youth had fought with bows and arrows, was in his old age the Minister of War of a modern army in a modern war. For the principles on which the development of the Japanese army was carried out they had at first to study the European armies and two opposite opinions prevailed, one party swore by France, and the other by Germany. At the time that the well-known General Meckel was acting as instructor in the Japanese Military Academy the last opinion carried the day. At the beginning of the War the instruction of the troops was conducted quite on German principles—they had simply translated the German Regulations for the Service into Japanese and in the same way they had endeavoured to model the General Staff according to German principles.

In this way our German principles for the command and the instruction of the army were tested in the War and we can be satisfied with the results. By their success, the Japanese were " Justified in the trust they had placed in our Military System."

After the War, when I presented my order of recall, I met General Fuji, the Chief of the General Staff of the First Army and told him I was anxious to know what changes in the Japanese Regulations would be introduced owing to their experiences in the War ; he answered, " So am I. We will wait to see what new Regulations for the Service Germany will issue on the basis of the reports that the officers who have been sent here will make, and we will translate these Regulations as we did the former ones."

I cannot close the chapter of my Japanese reminiscences without mentioning some of the foreign Military Attachés with whom chance had brought me in contact in the First Army of General Kuroki. They were destined to play special parts in the World War. Besides the well-known English General, Sir Ian Hamilton and Major Caviglia, who afterwards became the Chilian Minister of War, there were three Americans : Colonel Crowder and Captains Payton March and Pershing. They all three became celebrated in the new American Army that took part in the World War : Colonel Crowder in the organization department, Payton March as Chief of the General Staff and lastly, Pershing as

Commander-in-Chief. I was specially intimate with Captain March, who gave me English lessons, and who was exceedingly sympathetic to me owing to his intelligent military views and his straightforward and outspoken opinions.

As I have already said the Russians learned much from the Manchurian campaign. It is characteristic, however, of Russian conditions that these lessons were learned more owing to the initiative of a single person, than to the instructions given by the Central Department. General Rennenkampf, who had not distinguished himself very greatly as leader in the Manchurian campaign, wrote a scheme of new regulations for the infantry, based on his experiences in that campaign, which he first introduced in the Third Army Corps, and afterwards, when he became the Commander of the Military District of Vilna, he adopted it for the troops of that district. His scheme was then accepted, provisionally, for the whole army, but it never was properly drawn up in the form of Regulations.

When we considered in what way the Russian leaders were likely to make use of the bulk of their troops the correct and most natural method appeared to be, in our military judgment, to begin by throwing the greater number of troops against Germany. We were the strongest adversary; if they had succeeded in defeating us, the campaign against Austria would have been mere child's play. I therefore believe, if the German General Staff had had the disposition of the Russian Armies, that only those of the Kiev and Odessa districts would have been employed as a defensive force, all the others would have been sent against Germany. If the Russian High Command had arrived at this correct decision, many weeks would have had to elapse before the advance on the German frontier could have been undertaken ; that is to say, before all the troops including the Siberian Divisions could have arrived. We were as ignorant of the intended employment of the chief Russian forces as we were of the formations of the millions of trained soldiers, who were at the disposal of the Russian High Command. Until the Japanese War the Russians differed from the German and French opinion, holding that even in times of peace a certain number of skeleton formations were necessary, as cadres for the reserves. With the low standard of intelligence of the Russian soldier and the want of officers of the reserve and non-commissioned officers they could draw upon, such a standpoint was quite justified. For this purpose they had a number of reserve brigades. In the event of a mobilization by doubling them they could be formed into Reserve Divisions of the first order, and by quadrupling them Reserve Divisions of the second order.

Apparently Reserve Divisions formed in this way had not proved satisfactory in the Japanese campaign. I call to mind the check that Orlov's Reserve Division suffered at the Yentai coal mines. The Division came suddenly upon a Brigade of the 12th Japanese Division in the thick giauliang fields, which, with their long stems two or three metres high, hid everything from sight. The Japanese made a bayonet charge and repulsed the Orlov Division without their offering the slightest resistance. Consequently after the War the Reserve Brigades were disbanded and Reserve Divisions according to the French system and under French guidance were organized. We did not know how many of such Reserve Divisions had been organized, how long the organization had taken, or if they were included in the Reserve Corps.

CHAPTER II

THE RECALL OF THE GENERALS
VON PRITTWITZ AND GAFFRON

On the evening of the first day of the mobilization I arrived in Posen, the mobilization station of the " Army High Command 8."

This army[1] was under the command of Colonel-Generals von Prittwitz and Gaffron. The Woyrsch Corps had also to assist the extreme left wing of the Austrians in their offensive movement.

[1] It was composed of the :

    1st A.K. (General von François).

    17th A.K. (General von Mackensen).

    20th A.K. (General von Scholtz).

    1st Reserve Corps (General Otto von Below).

    3rd Reserve Division (General von Morgen).

    1st Cavalry Division (General Brecht).

    2nd (2nd Reserve Brigade) Landwehr Brigade.

    6th (2nd Reserve Brigade) Landwehr Brigade.

    70th (2nd Reserve Brigade) Landwehr Brigade.

Under the administration of this army there were included the deputy commands of the :

    1st, 2nd, 5th, 6th, 17th and 20th A.K., and the Eastern fortresses, and further :

    The Woyrsch Corps, composed of the Posen and Silesian Reserves, 20th and 1st A.K., that were stationed to defend the frontier.

These troops had the following areas for their advance :

    17th A.K., the district of Deutsch-Eylau.

    1st Reserve Corps, the district of Nordenburg.

    3rd Reserve Division, the district of Hohensalza.

    1st Cavalry Division, the district of Gumbinen.

    2nd (2nd Reserve Brigade) Landwehr Brigade, the distrct of Tilsit.

    70th (2nd Reserve Brigade) Landwehr Brigade, the district of Goster-hausen.

For this task it was positively insufficiently equipped ; above all there was a want of heavy artillery ; and, what can even be called a crime, was the want of proper medical equipment. The influence that the High Command of the 8th Army was able to have on the Corps was but small. The telephone connexions were bad, and became entirely disconnected as the Corps advanced owing to the want of material. I only succeeded twice, at the beginning, in obtaining a connexion with the Corps —a very agreeable surprise ! One of our most gifted and clever officers of the General Staff, Lieutenant-Colonel Kundt, who was my best friend, answered to my call. I had supposed he was in South America. Before the War he had gone on leave, with several other officers, to Bolivia, and just before the outbreak of the War he had obtained a furlough to go home and had arrived safely in Germany. Now I was glad to know that we had one of our most capable officers among our fellow-combatants.

Our army had orders to defend East and West Prussia against a Russian attack. At the same time it was to take care not to allow itself to be overpowered by superior forces or to be driven into the fortress of Königsberg. In the event of the advance of greatly superior Russian forces the instructions were to give up West Prussia East of the Vistula, and to take up positions behind that river.

The last portion of these Orders certainly contained great psychological dangers for weak characters.

However, the instructions, as well as the strength of the forces that had been destined for the Eastern front were no surprise to us as they corresponded approximately with our suppositions.

As is now generally known, according to the plan of campaign, which Count Schlieffen, the former Chief of the General Staff had worked out for a war on two fronts, the greater part of the German forces with a strong right wing was to advance on the Western frontier and, taking them by surprise, push through Belgium, envelop the Northern wing of the French army and roll it up. By these means the decisive action in the West was to be brought about quickly. The East during this time had to look after itself, and only when the decisive battle had been fought in the West could it expect support from thence. This plan was quite familiar to us, officers of the General Staff of Schlieffen's school ; we had played it out dozens of times in the War Game, and in Staff Rides.

The Commander-in-Chief of the army, General von Prittwitz, was well known to me as a clever, though somewhat harsh superior. I also knew very well the Chief of his General Staff, Major-General von Waldersee. Waldersee was generally considered a highly educated and able officer of the General Staff. At the beginning of the mobilization he was Quartermaster-General, and belonged therefore to the elite of the Chiefs of the Corps. Unfortunately at the time his physical powers were not equal to his mental, as he had but recently undergone a serious operation and his nerves were still suffering from its effects.

The first considerations that occupied the attention of the Chief of the General Staff and myself concerning the task that awaited our army were as follows.

We had no fear of the great Russian Cavalry invasion which was so much talked about ; our frontier guards would deal with that ; on the contrary it was to be desired that the Russians should effect such an invasion, and meet with a failure at once. We had first of all to reckon with the advance of the Armies, probably consisting of the troops from the Military Districts of Vilna and Warsaw (without the 17th Army Corps which was stationed on the Austro-Hungarian frontier). We could take for granted that their mobilization would be concluded by the 15th of August, so that we could expect the advance of both armies between the 15th and 20th of August, as the deployment would be made from the garrisons that lay near the German frontier and would not take long. It was doubtful if they would be strengthened by part of the troops from the Petersburg and Moscow Military Districts. Taking into consideration the Russian modes of military reasoning, it was possible to conclude that troops would be advanced somewhere in the neighbourhood of Grodno, as reserves and line of communication troops for both armies. But it was probable there could be no reserves yet in their appointed places, as their mobilization would require a considerable time.

On entering German territory the Russian advance would be divided by the obstruction of the Masurian Lakes. The Russians could only advance by sending one army to the North and the other to the South of this chain of lakes. Our army had therefore to be prepared to attack one of these armies, while they were disunited by the Masurian Lakes and defeat it. Which of the two would offer us the better opportunity could not be foreseen.

It could, however, be taken for granted that the army from Vilna would appear somewhat sooner on the theatre of war than the army from Warsaw, which would have to make its way through a district near our frontier, that was both boggy and deficient in roads.

Events proved the general correctness of our views. During the next few days the Russians made small cavalry attacks which were repulsed with ease. The Vilna army advanced in larger detachments with great energy on our Eastern frontier, while the Southern frontier of both East Prussia as well as West Prussia remained comparatively quiet.

The reconnoitering of the Warsaw Army was extremely difficult. The agents—Polish Jews— who during the first days had brought in news, failed us, as the Russian occupation of the frontier districts became denser. The Army had only one detachment of airmen at its disposal, which was obliged to restrict itself to flying over the communications that connected us with the frontier twice a day. Nevertheless that the Army would not so have been taken by surprise by the sudden appearance of the Warsaw Army, if the Russians had not been so cautious, marching only at night and keeping the troops under cover during the day-time.

The mobilization and the deployment of our Army was accomplished in accordance with our arrangements. The Army Headquarters moved on the 8th of August to Marienburg and from that day assumed the supreme command.

Before their arrival in Marienburg the Army Headquarters had trouble with the Commander-in-Chief of the 1st Army Corps, General von François.

As the Commander-in-Chief of the East Prussian Army Corps, General von François felt himself specially called upon to protect the province. It was quite natural that from his point of view he should make sure that no Russian should step on the soil of East Prussia ; and that no East Prussian village should experience the horrors of war. He was of the opinion that the task of the frontier defences was therefore to act offensively, and wanted by attacking the Russian Frontier Defence Detachments to keep them away from the frontier. He failed to see that by such tactics the 1st Army Corps would be removed from its contact with the rest of the army, and if the Army Headquarters had agreed to his plan it might easily have happened that the Army would have been obliged to support the 1st Army Corps on the frontier or possibly East of the Russian frontier and consequently the Army would lose cohesion and eventually might be obliged to fight on the other side of the Masurian Lakes, and thus forego the geographical advantages they offered. General von François made the mistake of omitting to inform Army Headquarters of his intentions ; so that Army Headquarters believed that the chief part of the 1st Army Corps was stationed on the Angerapp, while in fact it had been advanced much farther Eastwards.

Up to the 14th of August the information we were able to obtain about the enemy was that our opponent was advancing with strong forces to the North and the South of the Rominten Forest. He was developing especially energetic activity to the South of the forest. The Headquarters concluded, as they had already supposed, that the Vilna Army had advanced somewhat sooner than the Warsaw Army, more especially as the airmen's reports still continued to show that no movement of troops could be noticed on the roads coming from the South. The Chief Command decided to prepare the mass of the army for the attack of the Vilna Army.[1]

And in anticipation of the expected battle they moved, in the evening, from Marienburg to Bartenstein.

To his great astonishment, Major-General Count Waldersee received, on the 17th August, from the Chief of the 1st Army Corps a despatch from which it appeared that General von François had not executed the orders that had been given him, but had marched forward with the bulk of his troops and had brought on an action near Stalluponen. Both by telegraph and telephone the Army was ordered to break off the action instantly. The Quartermaster-General, Major-General Grünert, was sent in a car to General von François to transmit to him the order personally. Involuntarily this high-

---

[1] 20th A.C. was concentrated with its chief forces near Ortelsburg and held the frontier against advances from the South; on the right it was supported by the:

Frontier Defence Detachment of Dantzic at Neidenburg.

Frontier Defence Detachment of Graudenz at Lautenburg.

Frontier Defence Detachment of Thorn at Strassburg.

Also the 70th (2nd Reserve Brigade) Landwehr Brigade at Mlawa-Soldau.

On the Lake line, Nicolaiken-Lötzen, were stationed:

3rd Reserve Division with 6th (2nd Reserve Brigade) Landwehr Brigade.

1st Reserve Corps on the Angerapp with its right wing on the Mauer Lake.

17th A.C. was sent by train to Darkehmen.

1st A.C. was ordered to remain at Gumbinnen-Insterburg.

The chief reserves from Königsberg were dispatched to Insterberg.

1st Cavalry Division remained in advance of the left wing.

2nd (2nd Reserve Brigade) Landwehr Brigade held the Memel line at Tilsit.

handed action of General von François makes one compare it with the occurrences that took place in the Austro-Hungarian Army in the battle of Lemberg. There General Brudermann had also received an order to advance and to stop, and only to attack when he received an order to do so from the General Headquarters. Contrary to this positive order, General Brudermann attacked and by so doing contributed greatly to the loss of the battle of Lemberg. If it would have been possible to support him in his position by the energetic action of the High Command of the Army I am unable to judge. In the case of General von François it was possible to recall the Corps in time.

The battle of Stallupönen that was broken into in this manner was still quite a success for the 1st Army Corps. Superior Russian forces were repulsed and the Corps took many thousand prisoners. But all the same, with regard to the general position, it was a mistake. The 1st Army Corps, although the victor, had also losses, both in men and material, and chiefly in strength, which ought to have been husbanded for the great battle. Besides we had no interest in delaying the advance of the Vilna Army ; on the contrary the quicker it advanced the easier it would be to defeat it, before the Warsaw Army was able to make itself felt in the South.

In the meantime the deployment of the army on the Angerapp line was carried out as ordered.

The Commander-in-Chief of the Army went early on the 19th to have a consultation with General von Mackensen in Darkehnen, and then removed to Nordenberg.

In the afternoon of the 19th the High Command had the impression that the Russian troops that

were advancing to the North of the Rominten
Heath had come near enough and they gave the
order to attack.[1]

In accordance with this order the 8th Army
made the attack early on the 20th. Late in the
afternoon the engagement presented the following
picture :

Our right wing under General Otto von Below
had defeated the enemy that was opposed to it ;
the right wing under General von François was also
victoriously advancing. On the other hand the
centre under General von Mackensen as they advanced, driving the Russian vanguards before them,
had come upon a well constructed Russian field
position to the East of the river Rominten. Without
waiting for a sufficiently plentiful artillery preparation, Mackensen's troops attacked it, suffered severe
losses and were held up. The General Command
announced about three p.m., that the Corps was
defeated and that the position was serious.

The Third Reserve Division, under General von
Morgen, had been ordered by the Commander-in-
Chief to leave Lötzen about mid-day of the 20th,
as the position South of the Rominten Heath appeared not to be clear. Thus their assistance could
only be counted on early on the 21st.

Notwithstanding the check that Mackensen's Corps
had received the position of the battle was favourable

[1] The attack was to be made by the :
    1st Reserve Corps.
    17th A.C.
    1st A.C.
    The chief reserves of Königsberg.
    1st Cavalry Division.

The 1st A.C. was to outflank the North wing of the enemy, while the
3rd Reserve Division with the 6th Landwehr Brigade was to be ready
in Lötzen to make an outflanking attack on the enemy's left wing.

for the 8th Army. It could be reckoned that by continuing the attack owing to the outflanking of both the enemy's wings, a complete success would be attained.

About half-past six in the evening I was standing with Major-General Grünert before the office in Nordenberg. We had just been discussing the favourable prospects for the battle on the following day, when a message arrived from the General of the Artillery, von Scholtz, reporting that " the Russian Army from Warsaw with a strength of four to five Army Corps had begun to cross the German frontier opposite the front Soldau-Ortelsburg."

I remarked to General Grünert : " I am afraid the nerves of the Commander-in-Chief and the other chiefs are not strong enough to receive this message. I would be best pleased if we could suppress it. To-morrow we would end the battle here and then turn on our Warsaw opponent."

General Grünert answered :

" You surely would not keep back such important information from the Chief ! " He knew very well that I was not in earnest.

At that moment the Commander-in-Chief and the Chief of the General Staff came out of their quarters next to the office, and I saw by their faces that they had already received the message.

General von Prittwitz asked us to come into the office with them.

" Gentlemen," he said, " I see you have also received the message, and you know that the Russian Army from Warsaw will advance on our rear if we continue the battle, cut us off from the Vistula. The army shall therefore break off the fight and retire behind the Vistula."

General Grünert tried to explain his and my different standpoint : " that the battle near Gumbinen was in a favourable position ; that in two to three days we would be able to make an end of the Russian Army from Vilna ; and that it would then be time enough to turn on the opponent from Warsaw. Until then General von Scholtz and his Corps would have to manage for themselves."

General von Prittwitz cut short General Grünert's discourse abruptly, and said that he had decided to retire beyond the Vistula ; for the tactical decisions of the Command only he, and the Chief of the General Staff were responsible and not the first officer of the General Staff nor the Quartermaster-General." This was followed by orders given to me by Count Waldersee to make the necessary dispositions for the retreat of the army beyond the Vistula. I explained that I considered it would be impossible for the army to retire beyond the Vistula and I therefore requested to be instructed how the Commander-in-Chief wished the retreat to be effected.

Then the question of how the retreat was to be carried out was discussed. General Grünert and I showed, with the compasses, that a simple retreat beyond the Vistula would be impossible, as in order to retire in that way we would have to fight the left wing of the Russian Warsaw Army which was nearer to the Vistula than we were. That therefore it would be necessary to stop the advance of the Warsaw Army, and the easiest way would be by an offensive thrust at the left wing of that army.

General von Prittwitz, who as well as General Count Waldersee had for a moment lost command over their nerves, saw the necessity of the measures we proposed. However he stuck to his opinion that it was necessary to break off the battle against Rennenkampf, but he gave up the intention of retiring beyond the Vistula, and agreed with our opinion, that it was necessary to take up the offensive against the left wing of the Warsaw Army. According to these changed opinions orders were given on the evening of the 20th which formed the bases of the battle of Tannenberg. They were already created by them.

Orders were as follows :

The 20th Army Corps shall be concentrated behind its right wing in the neighbourhood of Hohenstein.

1st Army Corps and 3rd Reserve Division shall be sent by train, the first from Interburg, the last from Angerburg to the right wing of the 20th Army Corps.

Chief reserves Königsberg to cover the entraining of the 1st Army Corps and then go to the fortified line Pregel-Daime.

1st Reserve Corps and 17th Army Corps go direct back to the West.

On the arrival of the 1st Army Corps and the 3rd Reserve Divisions at the right wing of the 20th Army Corps, the advance of the Warsaw Army was to be checked by an offensive thrust of these three units against its left wing and flank. If, however, the 1st Reserve Corps and the 17th Army Corps were successfully detached from the enemy without the latter giving hot pursuit the Army Headquarters had in view a general reunion of the whole 8th Army in the neighbourhood of Osterode, with the intention of giving battle to both the Russian armies East of the Vistula. Whether it would be possible, and how it could take place, whether the action would be offensive against the Warsaw Army and defensive against Rennenkampf, or defensive against both could not be said at that time, as it principally depended on Rennenkampf's attitude.

I have lingered somewhat long over these details, as I consider it my duty to the memory of the deceased General von Prittwitz, to lay stress on the fact that the fundamental instructions for the battle of Tannenberg were given by him, because public opinion still only thinks of him as having wanted to lead the Army beyond the Vistula. He also had the intention of calling up the 1st Reserve Corps and the 17th Army Corps. That the possibility of the employment of these two Army Corps in the South could not have been reckoned with at that moment, must be quite clear to every military man, and even to every man without military knowledge : nobody could suppose that when, early in the morning of the 21st, Rennenkampf received the report of the German retreat he would remain inactive, everybody would have reckoned that he would have pursued energetically with all his forces.

The General Headquarters was informed, through a telephone conversation between General von Prittwitz and General von Moltke, of the first intention of drawing the army back beyond the Vistula, but not of the change in his decisions. The General Headquarters were not satisfied with this decision and recalled General von Prittwitz and the Chief of his General Staff, Major-General von Waldersee.

They were replaced by the Infantry General von Benneckendorff and Hindenburg and Major-General Ludendorff.

CHAPTER III

THE BATTLE OF TANNENBERG

IT is idle to ask the question : " Would it have resulted in a victory at Tannenberg if the Commanders had not been changed ? " I think : Yes— though perhaps not to so complete a victory, for the old chief commanders, as former experiences had shown, did not possess the necessary energy. There were at once difficulties with General François, and I do not know if the old Commander-in-Chief would have been able to get over them as easily as General Ludendorff did, and if he would have been able to support the strain that was put on his nerves during the next days by the question : " Will Rennenkampf advance or not ? "

The form of their recall was uncommonly rough. The subordinate Generals in command heard of it sooner than the Commander-in-Chief. Orders were sent by the General Headquarters to the Generals in command without the Commander-in-Chief being informed. For example, the 1st Reserve Corps and the 17th Army Corps were ordered to take a day's rest, the necessity of this order may easily be doubted.

The Headquarters had moved on the morning

of the 21st to Bartenstein and on the 22nd to Mühlhausen, in East Prussia.   The reports that came in announced that the retirement of the troops before the Vilna Army had been effected surprisingly well.

Colonel Hell, the Chief of the General Staff of the 20th Army Corps reported that the Corps had been successfully concentrated in the neighbourhood of Hohenstein, and he received the order to draw up the Corps on the line Gilgenburg-Lahne.   He expressed his doubts about the left flank of the Corps as it would take days to transport by rail the troops that were still on frontier duty, and therefore requested, that the 3rd Reserve Division should not be sent to the right wing of the 20th Army Corps, as the General Headquarters had ordered, but to have it sent to the left wing in the neighbourhood of Hohenstein.   This the General Headquarters approved of.

It was only in the afternoon of the 22nd that the Headquarters heard of the change in the higher command when a telegram sent to the Chief of the field railway announced the arrival of an extra train with the new Commander-in-Chief and the Chief of the General Staff.   It was only a few hours later that His Majesty's order arrived, which placed General von Prittwitz and General Count Waldersee on the unattached list.   General von Prittwitz bore this stroke of fate in an extraordinarily noble manner, and he took leave of us without a single word of complaint of his hard destiny.

On the evening of the 22nd a telegram from Ludendorff announced his arrival in Marienburg on the following day with the new Commander-in-Chief who expected to find the chief commanders there. When he sent this order, General Ludendorff supposed that the Army Headquarters was already West of the Vistula and wanted to have it transferred beforehand to Marienburg, but as the retreat that Prittwitz had meditated had not been carried out, he really ordered us back.

Hindenburg and Ludendorff arrived in the evening of the 23rd. General von Hindenburg, who afterwards became the idol of the German people, was up to that time but little known beyond the district of his old Corps. I had never seen him. Ludendorff, on the contrary, was a well known and often mentioned personage in the circles of the General Staff officers. His efforts to strengthen the army, which were only partially carried out in the great defensive plans, and also his endeavours to persuade the Ministry of War to have greater provisions of ammunition in store, in the event of a mobilization, which met with the same fate, were much discussed. There could be no question that the first success of the War, the important capture of Liége, was entirely owing to him, as was the general opinion of the army. At the beginning of the War he was Quartermaster-General of the 2nd Army under Bülow and had joined one of the columns—the 17th Infantry Brigade—that was appointed for the capture of Liége.

When the Commander of this Brigade, General von Wussow, fell, he succeeded to the command, and it was owing to his energy and activity that the fortress was taken ; while all the other columns failed more or less.

I personally knew Ludendorff very well ; we were at the same time General Staff officers at Posen, and from 1909 till 1913 had lived in the same house in Berlin.

General Ludendorff heard my report of the position, and approved of the measures that had been taken till then by the Chief Command.

The intelligence we had about the Russians reported that at least five Army Corps and three Cavalry Divisions from the front Soldau-Ortelsburg were advancing. Between Rennenkampf's army and our retreating troops there was a distance of about fifty kilometres, and Rennenkampf had made no efforts at pursuit up till then.

In the afternoon of the 23rd and in the early morning of the 24th, strong forces of the Warsaw Army attacked the left wing of Scholtz's Corps, the 37th Infantry Division ; after furious fighting they were repulsed with severe losses.

In connexion with this fight a small incident occurred—in itself of but small consequence, but which was of vital importance for the success of the battle. It turned out that the position of the victorious 37th Division had not been happily chosen and that a better position lay farther back. The Chief Command had gone early on the 24th to Tannenberg for a consultation with General von Scholtz. The General asked for permission to withdraw the 37th Division, after repulsing the attack, to the better position. The Chief Command agreed to this.

The voluntary retreat of the 37th Infantry Division proved to be a happy manœuvre : it aroused in the Russians the belief in a general retreat of the German army.

The enemy commander, General Samsonov, issued an order to the army to pursue. The order was sent by wireless from the Russian station, not ciphered, and we intercepted it. This was the first of numberless orders that in the beginning the Russians sent, with quite incomprehensible thought-lessness, unciphered by wireless ; afterwards they were in cipher. This thoughtlessness greatly faci-litated the direction of the war in the East, and in many cases even made the initiative possible for us. The cipher orders caused us no difficulties either ; we had two men on the Staff who proved themselves quite geniuses in deciphering, and in a very short time they found out the key to the new Russian code.

It appeared from Samsonov's order that in the advance of the Russian army, the 1st Army Corps, which formed the left wing marching on Soldau, should echelon sharply to the left and undertake the covering against Thorn. A similar order for the covering against Lötzen was given to the 6th Army Corps which formed the right wing and was to advance over Ortelsburg-Mensguth.

In the meantime General Rennenkampf's army remained stationary for some unaccountable reason. Only its cavalry advanced slowly, the infantry did not move. In consequence of this the Army Head-quarters turned the 1st Reserve Corps and the 17th Army Corps to the South, in order to bring about a decisive action against Samsonov.

The Army Headquarters ordered the decisive attack to be made on the 26th. Here again there were differences with General von François. General von François wanted to postpone the attack for one day, as some of his columns had not arrived and he also wanted the attack to be more far-reaching ; that is to say that it should extend in the direction of Mlava. In the opinion of the Army Command the time did not allow of this. Every day that we lost, might see Rennenkampf commence his advance and an outflanking of Samsonov's left wing near Mlava would only lead to a disunion of the 8th Army which was already very weak.

Order was therefore given to break through at Usdau—in my opinion the decisive point of the whole battle of Tannenberg.

On the 26th the 1st Army Corps with the assistance of Mühlmann's detachment (troops from the Vistula fortresses of about the strength of a mixed Brigade) had only succeeded in taking the heights of Seeben.

The right wing of the 20th Army Corps, the 41st Infantry Division, had on the same day driven the enemy back South of Mühlen.   South of Lautern on our left wing the 1st Reserve Corps and the 6th Landwehr Brigade had come upon the 6th Russian Army Corps which was advancing Northwards *via* Ortesburg and defeated it.

On the 27th of August the 1st Army Corps together with Schmettau's detachment of the 20th Army Corps stormed Usdau and drove the 1st Russian Army Corps Southwards beyond Soldau.

The 20th Army Corps had to defend itself from very strong Russian attacks.

The 1st Reserve Corps and the 16th Army Corps pursued the retreating Russians Southward beyond Ortesburg.

On the same day the Russians, not meeting any opposition, reached Allenstein.

I would like again to mention a little episode which shows what demands are made on the nerves of the leaders even during successful combats.

The Chief Command had been standing, till midday, on a small hill South of Gildenburg, whence it

had watched the storm of Usdau, and in the afternoon it had returned to the Headquarters at Löbau.
The reports that came in from all sides were favourable and the 1st Army Corps was advancing victoriously.

In Löbau we came upon columns and transport
trains of the 1st Army Corps which, to our surprise,
were going the other way and had turned their
horses' heads Northwards.

When in my astonishment I questioned the leader,
Cavalry Captain von Schneider, that officer explained
an order had come to make everything ready for a
retreat to the North.

When I got to my office, I was called to the telephone : the Commander of the ammunition column
and transport trains of the 1st Army Corps reported
himself from the station Montowo and gave me
the following information :

" The Second Battalion of the Grenadier regiment
has just reached Montowo, quite disorganized.
The Commander of the Battalion reports that the
1st Army Corps has been completely defeated and
it, as well as the 20th Army Corps, is retiring. He
had only been able to save himself and his battalion
from the general disaster by making a rapid retreat.
For all eventualities he had given orders to the
column to turn round with the horses' heads to the
North."

I did not doubt that this must be one of the
numerous panics that so often occur—but possibly
after we had left the field of battle the 1st Army
Corps had had to sustain a counter attack.

I next ordered the Commander of the Battalion
to come to the telephone, and I was very peremp-
tory. I ordered him to turn his battalion round

and to continue to march until he came upon the enemy. Then the Second Aide-de-camp of the Army Command, Captain Caemmerer, who afterwards became so well known as the personal Aide-de-camp of Field-Marshal Hindenburg, was sent in a motor with the order to drive on until he came upon either German or Russian forces.

Nevertheless, the next hour, while awaiting Caemmerer's return with his report, was a very trying one. This incident was soon explained. The Commander of the Battalion that had been sent to serve as a connexion between the 1st Army Corps and the Mühlmann Detachment had received reports that were partly false and partly exaggerated and believing there was an advance of strong Russian forces against his flank, he had lost command over his nerves.

On August the 28th, the 1st Army Corps with the 1st Division and the Mühlmann Detachment drove the enemy back beyond Soldau, while the 2nd Division and Schmettau's Detachment were already advancing on Neidenburg to envelop the Russians.

In the middle of the battle the Chief Command of the Army had ordered an encircling attack to be made on Hohenstein.[1]

Certain difficulties were caused, as the attack of the 41st Infantry Division at Waplitz had been repulsed by the Russian 23rd Corps. However, the advance of the 2nd Infantry Division on Neidenburg soon eased the situation. The 3rd Reserve Division (General von Morgen) supported by the von

[1] 20th A.C. and 1st Reserve Division from the West ; the Landwehr Division that had been transported from Schleswig by train and landed in Biessellen from the North ; 1st Reserve Corps from the West.

der Goltz Division stormed Hohenstein. The 15th Russian Army Corps called by wireless to its assistance the 13th Army Corps which was already advancing along the highway Allenstein-Grieslinen. Although by its attack the Landwehr Division of von der Goltz was brought for a time into difficulties, it was soon relieved by the 13th Army Corps being attacked in the rear by the 1st Reserve Corps.

The 17th Army Corps blocked the forest and lake districts in the East ; General von François, who rightly judging the position, had advanced his 1st Division on Neidenburg and had sent the Schmettau Detachment as far as Willenburg, completed the encircling movement from the South.

The fate of Samsonov's army was sealed. At least that was the opinion of the Chief Command in the afternoon of the 29th, and they ordered certain units, which seemed to be no longer needed for the last struggles to be ready to march away on the 30th August, to prepare for the imminent battle against Rennenkampf, when an incident occurred that might easily have had very unpleasant consequences.

On the morning of the 30th an airman's report reached the Army Command, as well as General von François, that the reinforced 1st Russian Army Corps was marching from Mlava on Neidenburg, and that its vanguard, at the time the message was sent was only about six kilometres distant from the troops of General von François that were stationed at Neidenburg.

The Commander of the Russian 1st Army Corps, General Artamanov, had rightly decided that by an attack on Neidenburg he might be able to break through the forces that surrounded them.

The Chief Command sent all the troops they could dispose of against this menace on Neidenburg.[1]

But at first the 1st Army Corps was without any support, and had to see how it could help itself in the difficult position. The energetic General von François was the right man to do so. He sent the Mühlmann Detachment against the flank of the Russian advancing Corps, and made a frontal attack on the enemy at Neidenburg with all the troops he could scrape together, without abandoning the encircling movement from the North.

The attack was repulsed after a comparatively easy fight. It is impossible now to decide if the enemy leader, after the heavy losses he had sustained in the fights round Usdau, had no longer the will for victory, or whether he feared an attack in the flank from the direction of Saberau, where the four heavy batteries of Mühlmann's Detachment had been firing very effectively.

The enemy Commander Samsonov shot himself when he realized the complete defeat of his army.

It is natural to ask, what were Rennenkampf's reasons for not coming to his assistance in spite of all the requests Samsonov had sent him by wireless. The explanation that his inactivity was caused by the very severe losses his army had sustained in the battle of Gumbinen, where some units had lost fifty per cent. or more of their effectives ; that the information he received only spoke of a retreat of the German 8th Army to Köenigsberg, and that therefore an advance of his army in a South-westerly

---

[1] The Landwehr Division von der Goltz ; the 3rd Reserve Division ; a detachment under General von Unger ; and a Division from both the 17th and 20th A.C.

direction would expose it to a flank attack from the fortress of Köenigsberg, are not sufficient to satisfy our military understanding. Every advance Rennenkampf could have made would have prevented the catastrophe of Tannenberg. I would therefore like to mention the reports, which cannot be quite disproved, that Rennenkampf did not go to assist Samsonov from personal enmity against him. We must naturally conclude that he did not realize what importance the effects of his decision, nor what the extent of Samsonov's defeat would be. I know that a personal enmity existed between the two men, it dates from the battle of Liauyang, where Samsonov with the Siberian Cossack Division was defending the Yentai coal mines, but notwithstanding the distinguished bravery of his Cossacks he was obliged to evacuate them as Rennenkampf, who was on the left flank of the Russians with his detachment remained inactive notwithstanding repeated orders. Witnesses told me that after the battle, there had been some very biting explanations between the two leaders in the Mukden station.

I remember that during the Tannenberg days I spoke to General Ludendorff about the feud between the two enemy leaders, and of my suspicions of the possible psychological influences that it might have.

On one of the last days of the battle of Tannenberg General Ludendorff summoned me to his telephone. He had been called up by Colonel Tappen, the Chief of the Operations Department of the General Headquarters. Ludendorff said to me : " Take the second receiver, so that you can hear what Colonel Tappen wants, and what I answer him."

Colonel Tappen informed him that three Army Corps and one Cavalry Division from the Western Army had been appointed to reinforce the 8th Army, and asked in what direction these troops were to be despatched. General Ludendorff gave the necessary instructions, but explained clearly at the same time that we were not positively in need of these reinforcements ; if the Western front found any difficulty in sending them the Corps might remain there. Colonel Tappen explained that the troops could be spared from the West.

The following day a similar scene was repeated. Again Colonel Tappen called us up—I had the second receiver of the field telephone—and he informed us that only the 11th and Reserve Guard Corps and also the 8th Cavalry Division would come, but that the 5th Army Corps which he had mentioned on the previous day was wanted in the West. General Ludendorff assured him once more, that the Corps would arrive too late for the battle that was then being fought, and that we were able, if necessary, to manage alone and therefore if the Corps was needed in the West to bring about a more speedy result the General Headquarters need not have any consideration for the East.

I wish to lay special stress on these two conversations because it has often been asserted that the General Headquarters had only decided on the " fatal dispatch " of these two Army Corps in consequence of the urgent demands for help from the East.

CHAPTER IV

AT THE MASURIAN LAKES

SAMSANOV's army had been practically destroyed. Of his five Corps three and a half were either dead or prisoners, the remainder about one and a half Army Corps, had to be sent back into the neighbourhood of Warsaw for re-formation. Our hands were free to act against Rennenkampf.

On the 5th of September the deployment[1] against Rennenkampf was concluded. His army had advanced by that time, and its right wing (about two divisions) had been brought up to our positions on the Deime ; about three Army Corps were stationed from that point along a line of Gerdauer-Drengfurth as far as Lake Mauer, the weaker forces of its left wing stretched Eastwards past Lötzen with detachments at Arys and Johannisburg.

The Russian Army had taken advantage of the delay to construct well fortified field positions.

[1] The forces were placed :

    3rd Reserve Division (von Morgen) at Friedrichshof.

    1st A.C. (von François) East of Ortelsburg on the roads to Johannisburg and Nikolaiken.

    17th A.C. (von Mackensen) at Mensguth.

    20th A.C. (von Scholtz) at Wartenburg.

    11th A.C. (von Plüskow) at Seeburg.

    1st Reserve Corps (von Below) with the 6th Landwehr Brigade at Heilsburg.

    Guards Reserve Corps (von Gallwitz) at Preussisch-Eylau.

    A.H.C. in Allenstein.

Landwehr Division Goltz and 70th Landwehr Brigade covered the right flank at Mlava and Myszniec.

To Rennenkampf's army belonged also four Divisions of Reserves, but I knew nothing about their individual formation. Shortly after, the Finnish Army Corps appeared on its Southern flank.

By papers that had been captured at Tannenberg the High Command had news of the so-called " Grodno Reserve." Besides the Finnish 22nd Army Corps, the 3rd Siberian Corps ought to have belonged to it, but at that time they could not be reckoned on, as the transports from East Siberia could not have arrived as yet.

The Chief Command had decided to make an attack on the whole front.

Three Corps (Scholtz, Plüskow, and Gallwitz) were to make a frontal attack, while Morgen, François and Mackensen advancing Southwards, past the Masurian Lakes, were to bring about the decision by an outflanking attack.

The 1st and 8th Cavalry Divisions were to be drawn on through Lötzen to the right wing in readiness when the decisive moment had been reached to be employed in the pursuit of the enemy.

The frontal attack did not progress, but the outflanking movement of General von François was decisive.

In a series of engagements on the 7th at Johannisburg, on the 8th at Arys, on the 9th to the North of Widminnen, he forced the Russian Detachments to retire, released General von Mackensen's 17th Army Corps from Lötzen, and by his enveloping pressure on Rennenkampf's right wing he obliged him to retreat.

Already on the fourth day of the battle the report of an airman had come in, who said he had the impression that the principal Russian positions were only feebly occupied, or not occupied at all, and on the following morning the Chief Command received the positive news that Rennenkampf did not mean to resist the attack, but had apparently given the order for a general retreat already on the previous day. Though this information deprived us of the hope of completely defeating Rennenkampf, I would not be speaking the truth, if I asserted that the news of his retreat was not very agreeable to us.

The frontal attack on the admirably planned positions of the Russians would have been very difficult. It appears to me doubtful if we should have been successful. It would only have been necessary for Rennenkampf to defend himself from the enveloping attack on his left wing by the three divisions of the Generals von François and von Morgen. Rennenkampf had for this purpose at the very least the Finnish Army Corps and six Divisions of his reserve. He could easily have turned this defensive into an offensive action. Even if our 8th Army had not suffered a defeat, it would not have been free for its next task—the support of the Austrians in South Poland.

On the receipt of the information that the Russian Army was retreating the Chief Command gave orders for its pursuit, to be carried out as follows:

1st Army Corps South East of the Rominten Heath towards Mariampol.

17th Army Corps North of the Rominten Heath towards Wistyniec.

20th Army Corps by Darkehmen, Walterkehmen towards Pillupönen.

11th Army Corps North of Darkehmen past Gumbinnen towards Stallupönen.

1st Reserve Corps by Insterburg towards Pill-kallen.

Guard Reserve Corps from Allenburg towards Gross-Aulowöhnen.

The Chief Reserve Königsberg towards Tilsit.

1st and 8th Cavalry Divisions were to go in advance of the 1st Army Corps towards the high road Wirballen-Kovno.

These orders were only partially executed.

On the morning of the 11th a report reached the Army Headquarters from the Chief Command of the 11th Army that it was being attacked by superior forces. The Army Headquarters already knew of the attack by a Russian wireless. From this it appeared only to be an attack by three regiments of a Russian Reserve Division. Although the Army Headquarters pointed this out to the Chief Command they insisted on the correctness of their report of the attack by superior forces.

It was quite possible that Rennenkampf might try, by a strong offensive attack, to break through and thus to prevent the pursuit of the 8th Army. The Chief Command allowed itself to be misled and ordered the 17th and 1st Army Corps to go to the assistance of the 11th Army Corps. This caused a quite unnecessary stoppage in the pursuit, and not-withstanding the strong insistence of the Army Command this loss of time could not be made up.

On the 17th of September there was a sharp rear-guard engagement at Wylkowyszki. Notwithstanding the skill the Russians displayed in the retreat, notwithstanding the want of consideration they showed by making the columns march alongside of each other on the sides of the roads, congestions occurred, more especially during the march through

Stallupönen. The rear guard was therefore sacrificed at Wylkowyszki in order to give the rest of the army time to escape. With this rear guard engagement the battle of the Masurian Lakes was finished. The chief merit of this great success must be awarded the Corps of General François and especially to the Reserve Division of von Morgen, who covered the right flank of François' offensive and defeated the Finnish Corps in many attacks.

Besides the liberation of East Prussia, this battle gave us the certainty that Rennenkampf's army was incapacitated for a long time. His losses in both men and material were very considerable, so that it would require weeks before it could reorganize while resting beyond the protective barrier of the Niemen and its fortresses. It is true Rennenkampf had not suffered a complete defeat, and I do not think that it would have been possible for us to rout him entirely.

An envelopment of both wings was impossible with the forces we possessed, and the conditions of the ground. Of course it would have been possible to have been more economical with the forces employed in the frontal attack, but if we had brought into action on the Deime the two newly arrived Army Corps—as General von François suggests in his book—only two Army Corps would have been insufficient to make an attack on a front of fifty kilometres.

We were quite ignorant of the strength of the Russian Reserve Divisions or of the recently arrived transports of fresh forces, so that every offensive they made might have had the most fatal consequences. On the other hand if the two Army Corps had made an offensive beyond the Deime sector they would have met with considerable difficulties. If the attack had succeeded Rennenkampf would probably have begun his retreat a day sooner, which the attack of these two Corps would not have been able to hinder.

On the other hand it is a disputed question whether it might not have been better to have employed another Army Corps to assist in the outflanking action on the right wing.

CHAPTER V

FOR OUR CONFEDERATE IN SOUTH POLAND

WHILE our army was fighting the battles of Tannenberg and of the Masurian Lakes the positions on the Western front and of the confederated Austrian army had developed unfavourably.

After the victorious advance of the German army in the West, on the 9th of September, General von Bülow had come to the fatal decision of retiring. We heard of what was happening in the West only by rumours. We knew that a reaction had set in and that the German advance had come to a standstill. Why and where this had happened, was not communicated to our Chief Command.

On the other hand more exact intelligence reached us of the unfortunate fights the Austrians had had near Lemberg and of their retreat beyond the San in the direction of Krakau. It was necessary to send to our ally the assistance to which he was entitled according to arrangements that had been made before the War between the Chiefs of both General Staffs. The General Headquarters therefore ordered us to furnish two Army Corps, and to dispatch them to Silesia. They were to serve there as the cadre for a new army under the command of General von Schubert and General Ludendorff was appointed Chief of the General Staff.

General Ludendorff went to Silesia, got into touch with the Chief Command of the Austrian Army, and was convinced that to send only two Army Corps was insufficient, and that energetic action was necessary in order to assist our ally, who had suffered much more than had been supposed at first. He proposed to employ for this purpose the chief part of the 8th Army under Hindenburg's command.

General Ludendorff's suggestion was carried out. The 9th Army[1] under the leadership of General Hindenburg was formed. General Ludendorff was Chief of the General Staff. Part of the Headquarters Staff of Army 8, including myself, was transferred to the Headquarters Staff of Army 9. General von Schubert undertook the command of the rest of the 8th Army which remained for the defence of East Prussia.[2]

The task of the Army that remained in East Prussia could naturally only be defensive. It was hoped that it would be able to keep the line Suwalki-Wylkowyszki, beyond the German frontier, that had been taken up after the battles near the Masurian Lakes. The last order given by the late Chief Command which I had taken to Wylkowyszki to General von François was at once to begin the

---

[1] The Guard Reserve Corps.
    11th A.C.
    17th A.C.
    20th A.C. and the Chief Reserves from Thorn and Posen which each had the strength of one Division.

[2] 1st A.C.
    1st Reserve Corps.
    3rd Reserve Division.
    Landwehr Division Goltz.
    Chief Reserves Königsberg.
    1st Cavalry Division, as well as a few Landwehr Brigades,

construction of a fortified position beyond the German frontier.

General von François had at that time no great opinion of fortified positions. He believed that the task of keeping the Russians out of East Prussia would be better effected by a few offensive thrusts. The order to construct this position was not executed, and only the construction of the Angerapp position which had been already commenced was continued.

There were several opinions about the way the 9th Army was to be employed. The Chief Command had at first intended that it should make an offensive attack from East Prussia on Sielce. Then an advance of the left wing from Thorn along the Vistula, in view of a subsequent advance on Warsaw.

During the first weeks of the War an offensive advance through Sielce had been demanded several times by Colonel-General Conrad von Hötzendorf. This offensive had played a considerable part in the correspondence that General von Conrad had had with General von Moltke before the war. Conrad had alluded to it several times as the most effective way of supporting the Austro-Hungarian offensive. It was now too late. The condition of the Austrian troops demanded immediate support. It was necessary to fight with them shoulder to shoulder at once.

Therefore the 9th Army received an order from the General Headquarters to get as near to the North of Crakow as they could.

The Headquarters of the Army went to Benthen.

On the 18th September General Ludendorff drove to the Austrian Headquarters at Neu-Sandec in order to consult with the Austrian Commander-in-Chief Archduke Friedrich and the Chief of the General

Staff Conrad von Hötzendorf about the operations
that were to be executed. He received a bad
impression of the condition of the Allied Army.
That the Austrians must have had enormous losses
in the battle of Lemberg and on the retreat from there
was the only explanation he could find for the
chief part of the Austrian Army, about seventy
Divisions, being crowded into the narrow space
on the West bank of the Wysloka between the
Carpathians and the Vistula. A large number of
the young officers and of the not too numerous
non-commissioned officers had fallen, a loss that was
irretrievable and from which the army was unable
to recover during the whole of the War.

From Ludendorff's account of the consultation
I received the impression that they were of one mind
about re-assuming the offensive as soon as possible.
For that purpose the 9th Army was to be reinforced
by the Landwehr Corps Woyrsch and the 1st Austrian
Army Dunkl, which were already under its control,
as they would soon have to cross to the North
bank of the Vistula. In Karl Friedrich Nowak's
book, *The Way to the Catastrophe*, which is based
upon communications and statements made by
General von Conrad, this agreement is denied.
General von Conrad's opinion was that at first they
were to act on the defensive and together form a
strong united front, and that afterwards step by step
an offensive would be developed from it. Although
I greatly esteem General von Conrad's vast knowledge and eminent capacities as a leader I cannot
share this opinion. The Russians had pursued the
Austrians with all their forces as far as the San ;
beyond the San inclusive of Przemysl with weaker
forces, but it was evident that this relief for the

Austrians was only temporary and caused by difficulties the Russians were experiencing in the transport of fresh drafts.   It was necessary to act quickly
and to free the Austrian Army as soon as possible
from being wedged in between the mountains and
the Vistula.   For this purpose the 9th Army had
if possible to compel the Russians to draw off strong
forces from the pursuing army and to bring them
into action against the 9th Army.   This was only
to be attained by active measures—by an advance
on the Vistula.

So far there were in the Government of Warsaw—
at least in that part of it where the operations of
the 9th Army were likely to take place—only a few
Cavalry and Cossack regiments.

The Chief Command of the Army did not doubt
for a moment that the 9th Army was strong enough
decisively to beat the Russian Army that was
opposed to the Austrians.

On the 27th September the 9th Army was ready
for operations.[1]

On the 29th September the advance began on the
line Opatov-Ostrowic-Ilza-Radom-Tomaszov-Kolisz-
ki to the East of Lodz.

At first the enemy offered no resistance.   Small
detachments of Cavalry and Cossack sotnias retiring
before our advance.   For the time all the information of the bulk of the Russian Army that we had

[1] 11th A.C. close to Crakau on the North.

Guard Reserve Corps, 20th A.C., 17th A.C., 35th Reserve Division
(Chief Reserves Thorn), between Kattowitz and Kreuzburg.

18th Landwehr Division (Chief Reserves Posen) and 8th Cavalry Division between Kempen and Kalisz.

35th Reserve Division, 18th Landwehr Division and 8th Cavalry Division were united under the command of the Bavarian General von Frommel
as the Frommel Corps.

were some wireless messages we had intercepted, from which we learned that the Russian Chief Command had recalled three Army Corps. The messages were, however, so old that they could not be connected with our present advance ; we supposed that these troops had been sent to support Rennenkampf's army when news had been received of the East Prussian disaster.

When the Russian Commander-in-Chief, the Grand Duke Nicolai Nicolaievich, saw that the 9th Army was advancing he came to a bold decision : he recalled about fourteen Army Corps from the main body of the army that was fighting against the Austrians and had the troops sent partly by train and partly by march route Northwards beyond the Vistula. Then the smaller part of the Army was to cross the Vistula and attack the German army in front while the greater part of the army reinforced by the Siberian Corps that had been detrained about that time in and near Warsaw, was to make an outflanking attack on our army on the line Novo-Georgievsk-Warsaw.

The idea was a good one. The Grand Duke had judged very rightly that it was necessary for him to get the 9th Army definitely out of action, and then to settle with the Austrian troops. Of course, at that time, we did not know his plan ; it was only by messages from the Russian wireless station, which continued to indicate to various Army Corps their positions, that we knew that considerable Russian forces were moving to the North of the Vistula.

The first effects of the Grand Duke's plan were very agreeable for the Confederates ; the Austrian troops were able to resume their march ; they were able to advance satisfactorily and on the 9th reached the San almost without any opposition and entered Przemysl.

Already on the 4th we had had a small engagement before Opatov with two Russian skirmishing brigades that had been sent by the Russian Guards Corps across the Vistula as their advanced guard.

The Guard Reserve Corps, which by advancing further East would have been in a position to cut these two skirmishing brigades off, allowed itself to be misled into attacking the enemy's left wing too soon, which caused the skirmishing brigade to make a rapid retreat.

Mackensen also had a small engagement with two Cossack Divisions near Radom.

In the meantime the Chief Command had realized that the Russians were withdrawing very large forces from the Austrian front to bring them into action against the 9th Army. It was natural that at that time the whole extent of the operations the Grand Duke Nicolai Nicolaievich intended carrying out was unknown to us. On the other hand, it appeared from the slight resistance that the Austrians had so far met with in their advance that it might be possible by an energetic offensive to inflict a serious blow on the Russians, while the 9th Army would hold in check the Russian forces that opposed them on the Vistula by a containing action.

It was therefore of importance to find out what the position at Warsaw was, and at the same time to prevent the Russians from crossing the Vistula with large forces between Sandomir and Warsaw.

The 9th Army was to advance considerably more to the North, and to extend its line as well as the line of the 1st Austrian Army, which was under its command, so as to cover the whole front from the mouth of the San to Warsaw.

General von Mackensen, under whose command Frommel's Corps was also placed, received orders to march Northwards straight from Radom on Warsaw.

As far as I can remember, there were no reports at that time of the detraining of Siberian Army Corps at Warsaw, as General Ludendorff asserts in his *Reminiscences of the War*. On the contrary these very rumours said that in Warsaw alone there were about 60,000 sick and wounded from the battles in East Prussia.

On the right wing of the Army the 38th Division of the 11th Army Corps was stationed at Annapol to give greater strength to the Dunkl Army and also in case of need to cross the Vistula later at Annapol, a good place for the purpose, if the Austrian offensive succeeded in crossing the San and in advancing.

Another Russian advanced guard crossed the river at Novo-Alexandre, and being attacked by us, was forced to recross it.

A Brigade of the 20th Army Corps came upon enemies who had crossed the river North of Ivangorod at Koschenice. The Commander of the Brigade probably over-estimated the strength of the enemy that had already crossed the river and hesitated to attack, in consequence of which the Russians —Caucasian troops—succeeded in establishing themselves on the left bank of the Vistula, and building a bridge. Notwithstanding all our efforts we were afterwards unable to drive the enemy, who fought with surprising bravery, from the left bank of the stream.

While marching on Warsaw, Mackensen's Corps that had been reinforced, came upon the enemy—

a party of Siberian skirmishers—at Grojec. After a sharp engagement they were defeated and forced to retire on Warsaw, pursued by Mackensen's Corps which on the 12th took up a position close to Warsaw on the South.

After the battle of Grojec an army order and sketch was found on the body of a Russian officer which revealed to us the whole of the Russian plan.

Mackensen was then sharply attacked by the Siberian Corps that came out of Warsaw. He repulsed these attacks.

The adversary again tried to cross the river at Kalvaria, South of Warsaw. He was forced to retire by the 37th Division of the 20th Army Corps. To the South of the 37th Division the other Division of the 20th Army Corps was stationed near the mouth of the Pilica. It was reinforced by an Austrian Cavalry Division. In touch with them was the reinforced Guard Reserve Corps. It was stationed opposite Koshenice and Ivangorod and cut the fortress off.

On the other hand, we did not succeed, as has already been said, in forcing the 3rd Caucasian Corps to recross the river at Koshenice. The weather was horrible at that time. It rained without intermission ; it was impossible to entrench in the saturated and flooded ground of the lowlands of the Vistula. The trails of the Russian gun-carriages were literally in the Vistula, but the Caucasians had set foot on the left bank and clung to it fast ; moreover, they even tried to gain more ground by constant attacks. These attempts were not successful, as every attack they made was driven back with great loss.

To the South of the Guards' Reserve Corps the

Landwehr Corps of Woyrsch was stationed opposite the bridge-heads of Novo-Alexandria and Kasimierz. At the last named place the Russians also made an attempt to cross the Vistula but they were easily prevented by the Landwehr Corps.

To the South of the Landwehr Corps the main body of the 11th Army Corps was stationed.

Thus the Russians had been prevented from crossing the Vistula, with the one exception of the bridge-head of Koshenice; the Vistula was barricaded between the mouth of the San and Kalvaria by the 9th Army and the position on this portion of the front was in general secured.

It was now only a question of time for the Russians to bring up more reinforcements and by making an enveloping attack on the Mackensen group from Novo-Georgievsk and the South-west they could have rolled up the whole front of the 9th Army—which was indeed what the Grand Duke Nicolai Nicolaievich had planned.

Mackensen had therefore to be reinforced, to enable him to hold out until the Austrian Army had been able to cross the San, and to achieve the success that General von Conrad still hoped for. The troops of the 1st Austrian-Hungarian Army were at our disposal for that purpose. There were two possible means of employing them: either the whole of the Austro-Hungarian 1st Army could be led behind our front to the North, and placed at the disposal of General von Mackensen, or it could be stationed on the Vistula, and thus release German troops which could be transported to Mackensen.

This movement would naturally have required time, and as time pressed the Chief Command was in favour of the first plan.

General von Dunkl, who had gone with the Chief of his Operations Department, Lieutenant-Colonel von Waldstätten, to consult with the Army Command at Radom, declared however that he had received strict orders only to allow his army to be employed South of the Pilica. Nobody in the Army Command could understand the reason for this order. Telegrams were sent to the Austro-Hungarian High Command and also direct to the Emperor Franz-Joseph, as well as through the intervention of the German Emperor to beg him to annul that order, and to place the Dunkl Army unconditionally at the disposal of the Army Command. All our endeavours were however in vain, the Emperor Franz-Joseph refused to interfere in the matter.

As an alternative General von Dunkl proposed that the Chief Command of the 9th Army should withdraw the German troops from Ivangorod, and that he should advance his 1st Army to the South of Ivangorod, facing the North. The Russians would then come out of Ivangorod and the Austro-Hungarian 1st Army would attack and defeat them. The Chief Command 9th Army would then be able first to dispatch the troops withdrawn from Ivangorod to Mackensen, and secondly General von Dunkl hoped that when he had beaten the Russians advancing from Ivangorod he would be able to obtain permission from his Army Command to employ certain units of his Army to the North of the Pilica.

While General von Dunkl was consulting with Field-Marshal von Hindenburg and General Ludendorff about these operations, Lieutenant von Waldstätten and I were exchanging opinions on the same subject. I drew his attention to the two defects

I found in the Austrian plan : first, it was not at all certain that the Russians would attack at once if we withdrew our troops from Ivangorod ; it might happen that the Austro-Hungarian Army would remain inactive, while Mackensen would be obliged to retreat owing to his left wing being outflanked. The second and more serious question was whether the Russians would not cross the Vistula with strong forces and that the 1st Austrian Army would not only not be successful but that on the contrary they would be defeated.

Unfortunately my fears proved to be correct.

In the meantime the danger that Mackensen's Army would be attacked in flank increased. The troops of the 1st Austrian Army advanced but slowly ; the relief of the German troops on the Vistula took too much time, and the Army Command found itself compelled to retire the left wing. This was effected on the line Mrava-Skerniewice-Lowicz.

The Landwehr Corps was transferred to the line Novoyasto-Mrava.

It was then possible to assemble the 20th, 11th and Guard Reserve Corps South of the Pilica. In the new front Mackensen's Group and the Landwehr Corps were to give battle to the pursuing Russian forces from Warsaw, while the above named three Army Corps were to make a united thrust to the North. For the success of this action the conditions were that the position in the rear of these three Corps should be secure : therefore, that first the Austrian troops which had relieved the 11th Army Corps and the Landwehr Corps should maintain the defence of the Vistula and that on the other side the chief part of the Austro-Hungarian Army that was stationed South of Ivangorod should hold the advancing Russians in check.

The danger for Mackensen's left wing had naturally not disappeared by this recapture ; the Russians had strength enough to be able to envelope him by a simultaneous frontal attack. This danger had to be reckoned with, as long as there was hope that the Austrian Army would defeat the Russians on the San.

Unfortunately this hope was not fulfilled. The Austrians did not succeed in crossing the San. On the contrary in the night from the 17th to the 18th the Russians crossed the San and attacked the Austrian 7th Army.

In the night from the 18th to the 19th Mackensen began to retreat. He succeeded in reaching the above mentioned position without any considerable loss of men or material.

On the 25th and 26th the 37th Infantry Division, the Landwehr Corps and the Mackensen group on the line Novomiestov-Lovicz were attacked in the most violent manner. The attacks were repulsed but Mackensen's left wing was obliged to bend back, and the Army Command found it necessary to recall to the South bank of the Pilica the 37th Infantry Division that was fighting at Novo-Miassto as the position of the Division had become dangerous owing to the river being swollen by the rains and there being only one bridge behind them which was exposed to the Russian artillery fire.

It was high time to act if the German troops that were stationed South of the Pilica were to make their offensive thrust to the North, but the first necessary condition, the safety of the rear of the troops was wanting. The second alternative that

I had suggested to Lieutenant-Colonel von Wald-stätten as possible had occurred. The Russians had advanced with strong forces from Ivangorod and their positions near Kosjenice; the Austrians had attacked and been defeated.

On the receipt of the first report that the advance of the Austro-Hungarian Army had become difficult and that the attack had failed, the Army Command again ordered the Guard Reserve Corps to make an attack in the direction of Kosjenice, in order to strengthen the left wing of the Austro-Hungarian Army.

On the 27th, about one p.m., a Lance-Corporal of our telephone section rang me up. During the change of the Headquarters of our Chief Command from Radom to Konskije he had remained with a part of our telephone section in Radom. He reported :

" I have just intercepted an Austrian Army Order which I think will interest you. The 1st Austrian Army is to begin a retirement at once ; but the German Guard Reserve Corps is not to be informed of this until six o'clock this evening."

I was naturally furious. I rang up Lieutenant-Colonel von Waldstätten, and gave him a bit of my mind. My protestations succeeded at last in obtaining the assurance that at least the left wing Division of the 1st Army would remain in position until we were able, when it began to get dark, to draw back our Guard Reserve Corps that was successfully advancing and about to attack in support of the 1st Austro-Hungarian Army.

In the meantime the 11th Corps was ordered to move to the North of Lodz to strengthen Mackensen's left wing in that direction.

With the failure of the Austrian troops before Ivangorod the whole position had become untenable. It was probable that the retrograde movement would also affect the units of the Austro-Hungarian Army that were stationed further South, and the 9th German Army would remain entirely unsupported. The 9th Army had also to retire, and to go back a considerable distance in order to attain the necessary power of action.

It has been asserted by Austrian writers and by some German ones too, that the retreat of the Austro-Hungarian 1st Army was caused by the defeat of the German Army before Warsaw, which had therefore been obliged to commence a retreat. This is not correct as I have shown above.

The cause of the want of success of our attack on Warsaw was that the Austrian Armies which were fighting South of the Vistula were unable to cross the San or to defeat the Russians who were weakened owing to having been obliged to send certain units for the operations against the 9th Army.

Now the 9th Army had to endeavour to escape from the Russians without their being able to pursue them too soon. As has already been stated the Army Command was aware at the time of its advance that the 9th Army would not be strong enough to achieve decisive success if the Russians opposed us with considerably superior forces. Already during the advance preparations had been made for the destruction of railways and roads in the event of the 9th Army meeting with a check, that might force it to retire.

The demolitions that had been arranged were now at the commencement of our retreat energetically carried into effect.

The retreat itself,[1] that had been ordered on the 27th, was carried out in perfect order and without any difficulties.

The Russians pursued us energetically along the whole front. They also attacked East Prussia and our frontier defences near Mlava. The position was serious on the whole of the Eastern front.

I quite agree with the opinion of our eminently capable Quartermaster-General Privy Councillor Dr. Keber, that the advance of a German Army would come to a standstill when it got about a hundred kilometres from the railway. We calculated that by giving the Russians an additional twenty kilometres, in consequence firstly of their exceedingly modest requirements, and secondly of their great want of consideration for their horses, we came to the conclusion that if we could succeed in destroying the railways so completely that it would require a long time to reconstruct them we should be able to stop for a time the advance of the enemy, who was pursuing us on Russian soil, to the East of the German frontier. We reckoned on a halt of several days. This period the 9th Army would have at

[1] The following units retired :

> Guard Reserve Corps, 20th A.C., Landwehr Corps to the district North of Cracow—North of Czestochova.
>
> 17th A.C. and Frommel's Corps to the district round Vielun.
>
> 11th A.C. to the district South-west of Sieradz.

On the left wing were assembled :

> 3rd Cavalry IV.
>
> 7th Austro-Hungarian Cavalry Troops IV that had been placed at our disposal, and also
>
> 5th Cavalry Division that had been sent from the West.

General von Frommel took the command of these three Cavalry Divisions, and the command of the former Corps Frommel was given to the leader of the 18th Landwehr IV—General Count Bredow.

The retreat of the Austro-Hungarian troops was chiefly carried out along both the banks of the Vistula towards Cracow. Weaker units retreated towards the Carpathians.

its disposal to begin new operations, and the time must be fully utilized.

Gradually the Army Command came to the conclusion that such operations could only consist of a concentration of a large portion of the Army in the neighbourhood South of Thorn ; the troops were to be transported by rail or to march there by road and they were to be reinforced by troops sent from East Prussia or from the Western front. They were to make an offensive thrust along the Vistula against the left wing and the left flank of the Russian army that was in pursuit of the 9th Army in the direction of Silesia.

That this permanent destruction of the railways and roads was successful was largely owing to the energy and circumspection of a very able officer of the Bavarian General Staff, Captain Sperr, who from the first had been entrusted by General Ludendorff with the direction of these measures.

In the last days of October General Ludendorff was summoned to Berlin for a consultation with General von Falkenhayn. And it was only there that the Chief Command became acquainted with the details of the events that had taken place in the Western seat of War.

CHAPTER VI

THE FIRST OMISSION

SCHLIEFFEN's original plan of operations was not carried out. He had intended that the left wing of the German attacking army should not advance, but on the contrary, should retire to the line Metz-Strassburg and the fortifications of the Upper Rhine before a possible French attack.

I do not know if Count Schlieffen had afterwards changed his plan of advance in any way, or if the alterations had been made under the direction of his successor. On this point it is only the two Chief Directors of the Operations who succeeded him there, the present Generals von Stein and Luden-dorff, who would be able to give any information. It is possible to suppose that the strengthening of the left wing of the German army was resorted to for the following reasons : At the beginning of the advance the great accumulation of troops on the right German wing must have met with diffi-culties. It was difficult to move several armies one after the other, without infringing on the neu-trality of Holland. It was only after the capture of Liége that space was obtained in Belgium and it was possible to allow a second and third army to follow each other in an echelon. If in the beginning a second and third army had been advanced in echelon on the right wing, it would have been quite possible during the first days of the campaign for these units to have been obliged to remain inactive on their place of deployment. It is therefore possible that the plan was adopted (with a view also of making equal use of all the railway lines) of sending a part of the troops destined for the right wing first to the left wing. It was probable that in the first days of the campaign the French would attempt to recapture Alsace and Lorraine by making an attack on those Provinces. An early success in this direction would without doubt have greatly raised the spirits in France and the moral of the French army. If this could have been prevented without interfering with the deployment of our own army, and our plans of attack it would certainly have been a practical move. It was possible to do so, if, as already mentioned, a part of the troops destined for the right wing had at first been sent to Alsace and Lorraine, where they would have repulsed the French advance, but then the troops would have at once had to be entrained and despatched for their real destination to take part in the offensive on the right wing. If these considerations were the causes of the weakening of the well-known Schlieffen Plan, or if there were others is, as I have already stated, unknown to me.

Judging by the conduct of the German Highest Command, this seems not to have been the case, as the strong forces of the left wing were left there permanently ; they allowed the battle of Lorraine to be continued by an offensive action of the 6th and 7th Armies and approved of the attempt to break through the French line of fortifications on the Mosel. This was certainly a conscious alteration of Schlieffen's original plan. Schlieffen wanted the decision to be attained by the offensive of a strong

right wing outflanking the French line of fortifications. If Count Schlieffen had considered that to
break through the French line of defence on the
Mosel was as easy as the Commander-in-Chief of
the 6th Army, General Tappen, seems to imply in
his work, *Till the Marne*, 1914, he would certainly
have laid before the Kaiser another plan of operations, and would have avoided the breach of the
neutrality of Belgium.

If Count Schlieffen's plan had been strictly ad-
hered to, troops would have been taken from the
left wing as soon as the Plan of Advance would
have permitted it, and sent by railway or road to
the right wing to follow it in echelon order. In
fact this operation only endangered the right wing,
which was to bring about the decision, and one
of the chief principles of military science is that in
a decisive action one can never be strong enough.
Not only did the Highest Command not send reinforcements to the right wing, but on the contrary,
during the further development of the operations,
took away from the right wing the two Army Corps
which they despatched to the 8th Army in East
Prussia without ever having been asked by it to
do so.

When General Tappen writes that the reports
received up to the 25th by the Great Headquarters
of the successes of all the armies had led the General
Headquarters to suppose that the great decisive
battle had already been fought in the West, and had
resulted in the success of the German army, this
seems incomprehensible. Even if the armies had
sent exaggerated reports of their successes—a general
and natural occurrence in war—the small number
of prisoners, the little booty that was taken, the

condition of the railways and roads, the absence of any signs of the retreat of enemy forces, ought to have taught the Great Headquarters a better lesson ; and when the excuse is given that the Chief High Command was too far in the rear, and they had to depend solely on the scanty reports from the armies, this certainly was their own fault ; they ought to have moved in time to the rear of the right wing— if the whole apparatus was too large, at least the Operations Staff might have moved—and they ought to have had constant connexion, not only with the different Army Commands but when necessary with separate General Staffs. This connexion they could easily have attained by liaison officers in motor cars. Both officers and motors they had in sufficient numbers at their disposal.

It is also incomprehensible that Lieutenant-Colonel Hentsch never received a written order for the mission on which he was sent, a mission that was of such vital importance for the fate of the whole German Army ; surely the Great High Command could have afforded to wait the ten minutes that a skilled officer of the General Staff would have required to write such an order. However the Hentsch mission has been sufficiently elucidated in the statement made by Lieutenant-Colonel Müller, Löbnitz. The question that Müller raises in his statement remains of permanent interest ; what would have happened if Field Marshal von Kluck, and General von Kuhl had refused to obey the order Lieutenant-Colonel Hentsch had brought them, and had insisted on the attack by the 1st Army which they considered right and meant to execute ? If they had done so, perhaps they would have become the national heroes of the campaign.

The total of the above-mentioned errors and omissions of the Great Headquarters led to the reaction of the Marne.

In place of Field-Marshal von Moltke who had fallen ill, General von Falkenhayn was appointed as Commander-in-Chief, and he had to decide how the operations of the German Army were to be carried on after the failure they had met with in the West.

It was quite right that the first thing that he did was to stabilize the whole of the front. But then he had to make a decision how the campaign was to be continued.

It is my opinion that there would still have been time to take up again the original Schlieffen plan. Ten Army Corps should have been transferred from the left wing to the right wing and with these united forces an attack might again have been made. If in consequence of this transfer the position on the left wing had become for a time more difficult, if large portions of Alsace and Lorraine had passed temporarily into French hands, that must have been accepted as a necessary condition, and it might even have had a good influence on the sentiments of the populace.

In August, 1916, when we were in Brest-Litovsk, General Ludendorff told me that General Gröner who had been at that time Chief of the Field Railways, had suggested a similar idea to General von Falkenhayn and he had even worked out a plan for the transfer by rail of six Army Corps from the left to the right wing. The suggestion was however rejected.

The Great Headquarters had therefore definitely given up all idea of carrying out Schlieffen's plan.

Why was it then that Count Schlieffen arrived at the idea of moving the greater mass of the German troops to the West and seeking a decisive battle in that quarter ? In the first place it was doubtless because here at quite the beginning of the War he would come upon the freshly deployed French army, who would be obliged to accept battle and would in no way be able to escape from him. During the first weeks of the war there would be no reason for a German attack on a large scale to be made on the East front. The mobilization and the deployment of the armies would take considerably longer and the Russian troops that would be at first placed in position could easily escape from a German attack by retiring into the endless depths of the Russian Empire, and without affecting the general position unfavourably by doing so.

It might have occurred to the Chief High Command if they felt themselves too weak to repeat an offensive on a large scale in the West, to try if it would not have been advisable to transfer the chief field of action to the East. The mobilization of the whole of the Russian Army was now complete. The question was only if in the near future the Russian Army would offer the possibilities for a great battle with the prospect of success for us.

Had it been decided to transfer the chief theatre of war to the East, it would have been necessary to release, as quickly as possible, troops in the West ; and likewise to give up the useless fighting round Ypres and by strict orders to force the troops to construct positions. Thus certain forces would have been released, and it would have been possible to wait for an occasion that required them to be brought into action on the Eastern seat of war. And the occasion presented itself.

CHAPTER VII

THE SECOND CHANCE

I DO not know if General von Conrad offered the same advice and proposed that after the failure of the German offensive in the West the chief centre of the war should be transferred to the East, or if he only asked General von Falkenhayn to send him local assistance to aid the German and Austrian Armies in extricating themselves from the difficult position they were in in Poland. In any case the Chief of the Austrian General Staff had asked General von Falkenhayn to send strong forces to the East. General Ludendorff related on his return from Berlin that General von Falkenhayn had refused this request as he required these forces at Ypres.

In the meantime the position of the German armies on the Russian front had become very serious. The 8th Army in East Prussia had fought with varying success against the Russian forces, and had till then been able to maintain its position on Russian soil. The Chief High Command had sent it the 25th Army Corps that had been formed according to plan, but which like the reinforcements that had been sent to the West suffered from the same complaint, that it was composed on the one side of enthusiastically patriotic, but quickly and insufficiently trained soldiers and on the other side of old officers and non-commissioned officers who were physically no longer fit to support the fatigues of the campaign. Our Ministry of War also recognized this organic defect and later new units were formed on a different basis.

It was sad to see that a part of our best youth was sacrificed in this way and a feeling of anger is aroused when one thinks how these young men who were glowing with love for the Fatherland, went with songs to meet an objectless death at Ypres.

The 8th Army was also strengthened by new formations from the fortress of Königsberg. In the same manner Zastow's Corps of the strength of about two Divisions was formed in the neighbourhood of Soldau of the garrisons of the Vistula fortresses and the Landsturm (3rd Reserves).

With energetic vigour General Ludendorff drew from the Eastern fortresses all that could be extracted from them for the reinforcement of the 9th Army. From Posen, exclusive of the 18th Landwehr Division, which was already in the field a whole Corps under General von Koch was drawn. That this was possible and in so short a time is thanks to the special merit of Colonel Marquard, the Chief of the Staff at Posen, who unfortunately died too soon. The fortress of Thorn, whose Chief Reserve, the 35th Reserve Division, was also already fighting in the open field, had to give up its 2nd Chief Reserve, the so-called Westerhagen Brigade, that already, during the advance of the 9th Army on the Bskura, had been pushed forward, but during the retreat had been recalled to Thorn. From this Brigade the Dickhuth Corps was afterwards developed.

Like Posen, Breslau was also to provide a Corps but here the formation progressed slowly and the requisite strength was never attained.

On the whole of the Eastern front we had to expect fighting as our retreat from Warsaw was naturally celebrated as a victory by the Russians and a great impulse was given to the whole of the Russian Army to make an energetic advance.

The Russians followed the 9th Army as quickly as the destroyed ways of communication would allow. They attacked vigorously in East Prussia, and there was fighting also with Zastrow's Corps near Mlava.

General Ludendorff had not concealed from General von Falkenhayn the seriousness of the position, and had specially emphasized that, in his opinion, the Russians would now try to bring about the decisive battle of the campaign on the whole of their front. It was urgently necessary, before all things, to have a single Chief Command on the Eastern front in order to provide reinforcements for the weaker points, at least for the most important places. In consequence of his report the post of " Commander-in-Chief of the East " was created. On the 1st of October, H.M. the Kaiser appointed Field-Marshal von Hindenburg as Commander-in-Chief of all the fighting forces on the Eastern seat of war. General Ludendorff became Chief of the General Staff. As the oldest officer on the General Staff, I also went over to the new formed staff. General von Mackensen was appointed Commander-in-Chief of the 9th Army and General Grünert became the Chief of his Staff. Lieutenant-Colonel Kundt was my successor.

In the meantime our calculations of how far the

Russian Army would be able to follow us without a railway proved to be correct. At the distance of 120 kilometres from the railhead the wireless of the Russian Corps announced that they were unable to continue the pursuit.

The Army had now a few days to reorganize before recommencing active operations.

In the meantime, after long consultations and deliberations the plan for the new operations had gradually crystallized. It was decided that the left wing should advance from the direction of Thorn along the Vistula to encircle the right wing of the Russian army that had followed us from Warsaw, and to defeat it. The chief part of the 9th Army was to be sent by railway and road towards the North and to be strengthened as much as possible by forces sent from the 8th Army in East Prussia. In place of the 9th Army that had been transferred Northwards other troops had to occupy their former front, otherwise the Province of Silesia, with its mines, would be open to an invasion, if only a temporary one, by the Russians. Here Field-Marshal von Conrad came to our assistance.

This man of genius saw at once the correctness of the intention of making an attack from Thorn and also the necessity of employing all the forces of the 9th Army for it. He declared he would assist the undertaking with all the powers at his command. He transferred by railway the whole of the army of Böhm-Ermolly from the Carpathians to replace the 9th Army in the neighbourhood North of Czestochova. If the German High Army Command had only shown a similar appreciation of the plans of operation formed by the Commander-in-Chief in the East, it would most probably have been possible to strike a decisive blow at the Russian Army.

In the first place, it was much to be desired that besides a reinforcement for the advance made from Thorn that the forces of Zastrow, near Mlawa, should be strengthened.   If it were possible to make an offensive from here at the same time as the attack from Thorn, if even with weaker forces, it would be possible to hold back at least the forces stationed to the North of the Vistula from taking part in the battle that was desired to take place to the South of the Vistula.   Unfortunately the wish placed only a few Cavalry Divisions at our disposal.[1]

[1] From the 8th Army the 1st Reserve Corps, General von Morgen, and the 25th Reserve Corps, Freiherr von Scheffer-Boyadel, were sent to Thorn. The last unit had unfortunately suffered very much in the previous fights in East Prussia, and came in a low condition and with an insufficient number of officers, so that it could not be looked upon as ready for action.

20th A.C. and 3rd Guard Division, General Litzmann of the Guard Reserve Corps, were sent by railway to the district South of Hohensalza, 17th A.C. to the district South of Gnesen.

In the same place were concentrated the Cavalry Corps of Richthofen, 6th and 9th Cavalry Divisions.

11th A.C. marched along the frontier in German territory in neighbourhood of Wreschen.

South of this point between the Prosna and the Warthe the Cavalry Corps of Frommel was stationed in close touch with the Cavalry Corps of Novikov.

Behind the Cavalry Corps of Frommel the Corps from Posen was advancing.

Farther South Landsturm (3rd Reserve) and the Breslau Corps, that was being formed, were stationed.

From Bielun up to the South of Czenstochova-Kamen was the remaining part of the 9th Army under General von Woyrsch, viz. :

    35th Reserves—IV.

    Landwehr—IV, Count Bredow.

    The Landwehr Corps and the Guard Reserve Corps without 3rd
        Guards—IV.

In the area North of Czestochova the Army of Boehm-Ermolly then squeezed in.

The wish of the Commander-in-Chief in the East to release all the units of the 9th Army could not be realized.   The morale of the Austro-Hungarian Army was not over good and General von Conrad was therefore of the opinion that it would be necessary to leave those German troops that were still in the neighbourhood of Czestochova, if the Commander-in-Chief in the East wished to have the co-operation of the Austro-Hungarian Army in the offensive North of the Vistula.

The Commander-in-Chief in the East transferred his Headquarters to Pösen on the 1st of November ; the Chief Command of the 9th Army took up its quarters in Hohenzalza.

On the 10th of November the 9th Army was ready for operations.

In the meantime the Russians had continued their offensive in East Prussia and round Mlawa.   The 8th Army being weakened by having had to give up two Corps was unable to hold the German frontier. A change in the command had also taken place during this time.   General von François, from personal reasons, had petitioned to be relieved from the Chief Command.   General Below, one of the most capable leaders of the War, succeeded him.

He led the Army back to the fortified lines of the Masurian Lakes and the river Angerapp and from thence repulsed every attack of the Russians. Zastow's Corps was also obliged to retire to the positions on the line Soldau-Neidenburg.   This line was retained.

The enemy who had pursued us from Warsaw, was stationed with its weaker part round Wloclawek and the chief forces from Sieradz over Novo-Radomsk to the area East of Cracow.   He was unable to advance from that line owing to the disorganization of his communications, but his wireless messages told of his being able to do so within the next few days. It was therefore high time for the 9th Army to begin operations.

At that time General Ludendorff applied again to the Chief High Command, explained to them what good prospects of success the proposed operations presented and requested General von Falkenhayn by desisting from the attacks on Ypres, to be able to send reinforcements to the East. The Chief High Command promised reinforcements, but we only received gradually information as to the number of troops we could expect or the time when they would be sent. Although it was very desirable to postpone the commencement of operations until these reinforcements arrived and then to deal a heavy blow with them, however proved impossible. As I have already mentioned, we had to expect a renewed Russian attack in a few days ; the time that fate had given us to make preparations for the new operations had expired—we were obliged to act with the forces we had at our disposal.

The High Command of the Army ordered the advance for the 11th November.[1]

The Russians were taken entirely by surprise. There was sharp fighting at Wloclawek, Kutno and

---

[1] The following units were to advance :

The Posen Corps on Sieradz-Lask.

Frommel's Cavalry Corps North of Sieradz on Lödz.

11th A.C. *via* Kolo on Dombe.

17th A.C. towards Lenezyce.

20th A.C. and 3rd Guard Division from the area South of Hohensalza towards Kutno.

25th Reserve Corps and 1st Reserve Corps *via* Wloclawek and South of Lowicz.

The Breslau Corps was to join up to the South of the advancing army.

Dombe, in which our troops remained victorious and drove the enemy back with heavy losses.

Then the left wing of the Army was sent forward to make an enveloping attack on the Russian forces at Lödz. The Generals Baron von Scheffer-Boyedel, Leitzmann, von Scholtz, and Baron von Richthofen broke through the line Lödz-Lowicz and forced their way victoriously to the rear of the Russians in the district of Brzeziny, while Plüskow and Mackensen made a frontal attack and stormed Lödz. The left flank of the Army was covered by General von Morgen with the 1st Reserve Corps in the area North of Lowicz. At that place he had several engagements with the Russian forces which had advanced from the Northern bank of the Vistula, they having crossed it at Novo-Georgievsk and West of that town.

They advanced singly and were defeated in turn by General von Morgen. However in consequence of their attacks General von Morgen was unable to reach Lowicz and the district South of it in time also to cover the outflanking movement against Warsaw.

General Scheidemann, the Russian Commander at Lödz, sent constant reports by wireless of the desperate position he was in, but continued to defend himself furiously.

It was on the 18th—if my memory does not deceive me—that we intercepted a Russian wireless message that ordered the retreat of the Russian army from Lödz. Instructions were at once given to the Army to pursue ; unfortunately it turned out otherwise ; the Grand Duke Nicolai Nicolaievich annulled the order to retreat and ordered the army to remain where it was.

Plüskow's Corps, supposing that there was to be a pursuit, had advanced and suddenly came upon advancing Russians and found itself in a very difficult position.

In the meantime the victorious outflanking wing of the Army had reached the district South-west of Brzeziny, and turning Westwards was preparing to advance in the rear of the enemy at Lödz. General Baron von Richthofen's Cavalry had pushed forward almost as far as Petrikau Tomaschow. If the movement was not interrupted from the direction of Warsaw great things could be expected from it.

The Commander-in-Chief in the East had warned the 9th Army very seriously of the danger that might be expected from Warsaw and had more than once advised that Lietzmann's Guard Division should be left at Skiernewice. The High Command had probably hoped that General Morgen would have been able to push through to Lowicz sooner than he did and cover the attack on Warsaw. The enveloping wing was also instructed to secure itself against attacks from Warsaw at Skiernewice; apparently the Great Headquarters had given this order too late and it never reached the leader of the enveloping troops. The Great Headquarters was too far in the rear: it had remained in Hohenzalza instead of following the wing of its Army that was to bring about a decision.

Thus at the moment we had hopes of a great success, a serious reaction took place. Between the left wing of General von Scholtz's Army and the forces that were advancing in the rear of the enemy, the communications were suddenly broken off; Russian troops had pushed in between them. At the same time the Russian leader succeeded in getting

F

a new Division to march out of Warsaw, over Skiernewice, which together with the troops that had remained there at the time of the German break through now advanced on Brzeziny. Richthofen's Cavalry Corps which was advancing from the South for the support of Scheidemann's Army was driven back.

The 25th Reserve Corps, the 3rd Guards Division and Richthofen's Cavalry Corps were cut off and surrounded by the Russians. The Russian wireless triumphantly announced the expected great success. The Russian Command was counting quite positively on the capture of these units. Orders were given by wireless for the preparation of some sixty empty trains for the transport of the hoped-for German prisoners—when in the night from the 24th to the 25th the German troops broke through victoriously to the North.

Every unbiassed critic must unquestionably award the chief merit of this success to the Commander of the 3rd Guards Division, General Lietzmann.

After having broken through the lines these troops took up positions in the front between von Scholtz's Corps and Morgen's Corps. The Commander-in-Chief in the East had also the 1st Infantry Division of the 8th Army brought up from East Prussia. Notwithstanding the small number of his troops General von Below gave them unhesitatingly. In this way a connected line was formed which the Russians vainly tried to break.

Although in this way greater misfortune was avoided, the great tactical success we had striven for was not attained.

Already in the middle of November the Austro-Hungarian Armies, together with the Woyrsch's

Army Detachment had begun an offensive to the South of our positions ; in the beginning they progressed very well, but soon had to pause and were brought to a standstill as soon as the Russians commenced a counter attack.

From the beginning of December the promised reinforcements began to arrive from the West.[1]

These reinforcements did not arrive simultaneously but in detachments.

At the request of General von Conrad, Gerok's Corps, the 47th Reserve Division, was sent to the Austro-Hungarian front and took a prominent part in the fine success they had at Limonovo.

The arrival of these reinforcements gave the front a new impulse to advance. Lödz was taken on the 6th of December and the Russians were driven back beyond the sector of the Ravka and the Bzura.

I would like here to mention a small episode which I think is worth preserving in history although it is not of a military nature. On the day Lödz was taken the Chancellor of the Empire, von Bethmann-Hollweg, paid us a visit in Posen. After dinner the conversation turned on the question of peace, and especially how it could be attained. Asked by the Chancellor for my opinion, I said that to my belief the first condition, even before peace could be talked of, would be for Germany to publicly declare by the mouth of the Chancellor of the Empire, that we did not want to keep a single square yard of Belgian land, as England would never tolerate a

[1] 3rd Reserve Corps (General von Beseler) and 13th A.C. (General von Fabeck) were brought into action on the left wing of the 9th Army.

2nd A.C. (General von Linsingen) was stationed to the East of Sieradz.

27th Reserve Corps (General von Gerok) reinforced the Breslau Corps.

German Belgium and would fight to the bitter end to prevent it. Besides I thought an expansion by Belgian subjects was not at all to be desired for Germany. The Chancellor replied : " You are the first soldier from whom I have heard this opinion. I quite agree with your point of view. But if I tried to express it in Berlin in the Reichstag, the storm of public opinion would sweep me from my post." I felt deeply affected by the thought that the Chancellor of the German Empire could not dare to say something that he thought was right for the German people from fear of being obliged to vacate his Ministerial seat !

The Command in the East has been blamed for having sent to the front the troops that came from the West as they arrived, as it would have been better to have brought them into action all at the same time in order to attempt once more the operation of outflanking the Russian Northern wing. I do not think, after the moment of surprise that had assisted us in our attack from Thorn was passed that we could have achieved much more, while on the other hand without the rapid reinforcement of the line as the troops arrived many points held by the 9th Army would have remained in a somewhat critical position.

Naturally it would have been otherwise if the German High Command had realized that the fortunes of war were offering them the possibility of giving the Russian Army such an over-powering blow that it would never have been able to recover from it afterwards. If it had desisted at the proper time from the little fights round Ypres and had taken from thence and from other points of the front troops for the East, and had decided to make a grand attack on that front, there would have been a certain prospect of such a success.

Let us suppose that the arrival of reinforcements from the West had come in sufficient time, that they would have prevented the reaction at Brzeziny and that the outflanking movement against Scheidmann's army had fully succeeded, the bulk of the Russian Army would have been squeezed together in the bend of the Vistula. The greatness of the Russian defeat could have been increased if at the same time as the outflanking movement from Lödz was begun, an attack had been made towards Warsaw by several Army Corps from the direction of Mlawa, on the other side of the Vistula. At that time the Command of the Russian Army would have sent all the stronger forces from the North bank of the Vistula to the South bank, to repulse the attack of the 9th Army. It had been possible for the Landsturm of Zastrow's Corps, strengthened only by the 2nd and 4th Cavalry Divisions to penetrate as far as the line Ciechanow-Przanysz. An advance of two or three strong Army Corps would have found it easy to reach Warsaw and the Great Warsaw Railway, which was the chief line of communication for the Russian Army. The results of such an operation are scarcely to be imagined. At that time the Chief of the Operations Staff Colonel Tappen, while passing through the town stopped at Posen, and I saw him in his railway compartment, where I implored him, almost on my knees, to persuade the Commander-in-Chief in the East to put at our disposal, besides the promised reinforcements at least two Army Corps more for such an attack from Mlawa-Warsaw, but it was refused.

In my opinion the campaign in South Poland is the finest operation of the whole War ; the rush from Cracow towards the Vistula to relieve our Confederates, the retreat on Czenstochau, the throwing of the Army from there to Thorn, and the renewed attack on the right wing of the fleeing Russians are, as operations, to be classed much higher than the plan for Tannenberg or any other of the victorious battles of the Eastern front. It is lamentable that the Highest Army Command lost this chance of allowing this fine operation for a decisive success to come to maturity.

Although the operations of the 9th Army and the Austro-Hungarian Armies were not able to go as far as the Carpathians, that is the decisive success was denied them, which would perhaps have aroused in the Tzar the wish to approach the question of Peace, still they resulted in preventing the " Russian steam roller " from entering Silesia and Posen and eventually brought it to a standstill. The enemy was driven back into their well known permanent positions which they were never able to leave afterwards. Unfortunately parts of East Prussia had to be abandoned to the Russians.

General Borocvicz's attempts to come out of the passes of the Carpathians between Dunajek and San and press upon the Russians' front soon had to stop as the Russians again began to advance and the chief point of their attack was directed against the left wing, consequently against the passes of the Carpathians.

CHAPTER VIII

RUSSIA'S GIGANTIC PLAN OF ATTACK

THE 9th Army in their permanent positions on the Ravka and the Bzura were continually engaged for several weeks, but in spite of this, the Commander-in-Chief in the East had a feeling of temporary quiet and relief.

The troops had an aversion to the construction of trenches, and a war of position, and it required the whole of General Ludendorff's energy to get them under ground ; in any case the construction of fortified positions was sooner resorted to in the East than it was in the West.

After the construction of the positions it was possible to take considerable forces from the front of the 9th Army and to employ them in other ways. Some were used on the frontier of East Prussia, and others were sent to support our Allies in the Carpathians.

Unpleasant news came at this time from Servia. General Potiorek, deceived by his first successes, had allowed himself to be completely defeated by the Servians.

The Russian High Command wished by a great offensive against its two opponents, to bring the War to a decisive end in the Spring of 1915. The number of its units that had now arrived at the theatre of war, the enormous masses of thoroughly trained troops that it had at its disposal to fill up the gaps caused by losses, permitted it to attempt decisive battles at the same time in the North and in the South; in the South against the passes of the Carpathians, in the North against East and West Prussia.

General von Conrad had the intention of meeting the Russian attack by an offensive from his side, and at the same time to relieve the fortress of Przemysl that had again been surrounded after the Austrian retreat from the San; he brought up all the forces he could dispose of and formed a new army under General von Pflanzer-Baltin in the Bukowina, but at the same time he asked for German reinforcements. General Ludendorff was in favour of sending these reinforcements, even if they had to be sent by the Commander-in-Chief in the East. These reinforcements were formed of three new Divisions of the German Southern Army under General von Linsingen and dispatched into the neighbourhood of Munkacz, where four Austro-Hungarian Divisions were also placed under von Linsingen's orders.

General Ludendorff was sent to be the Chief of the General Staff of the new Army for a time. The object of this measure was not very evident. The Southern Army had already a Chief in General von Stoltzmann; General Ludendorff was placed above him as First Chief of the General Staff. The Army was too small for such a prodigality in staff officers. It appeared to us on the Staff of the Commander-in-Chief in the East that it was only done to separate General Ludendorff from General Hindenburg, who in the meantime had been appointed Field-Marshal, as these two personages had become as one in the mind of the populace. Field-Marshal von Hindenburg protested against being deprived of his Chief of Staff in a report he sent to H.M. the Kaiser, and succeeded in getting General Ludendorff back after a few weeks, and before the beginning of the winter battles in the Masurian district. During his absence I was entrusted with the business of Chief of the General Staff.

At first we naturally knew nothing of the Russian plans against the Germans; we only heard through various wireless messages and also by the reports of our agents of a " gigantic " plan for an offensive against East and West Prussia. It was only later that the reports crystallized, and we learned that in the beginning of the year 1915 the Russians intended to make an outflanking attack from the North on East Prussia while at the same time strong forces were to attack the German weak positions at Mlawa, and entering from the South, to penetrate into Prussia.

The Prussian Ministry of War was forming four new Army Corps within the country. The first new formations had taught it experience and these Corps were composed in a more practical manner. They were given a sufficiently strong parent unit of trained non-commissioned officers and men and an adequate staff of efficient officers. Unfortunately the number of such officers was already becoming scanty in the Army. The first battles, especially in the West, had left enormous gaps in the effectives among Lieutenants and Captains, which could never be made good afterwards.

The Commander-in-Chief in the East made it clear to the General Headquarters that he required the four new Corps to be placed at his disposal.

On the one hand he was expecting the great Russian attack on East Prussia, and the forces he had would certainly be insufficient to oppose it, and on the other hand East Prussia was demanding very justly to be released from the Russian occupation.

On the occasion of a short visit that the Minister of War and the Chief of the General Staff, von Falkenhayn paid to Posen, I had the opportunity of repeating this pressing demand verbally and at the same time to explain how the Commander-in-Chief in the East proposed to employ these four Corps. It was planned that three of these Corps should be sent to the left wing of the 8th Army close to the South bank of the river Memel to envelop and roll up the free North wing of the Russian Army. At the same time the fourth Army Corps that was put at our disposal reinforced by an Infantry Division from the 8th Army was to break through the evidently weak left wing of the Russian Army South of the Masurian Lakes, or drive them back, and in this way outflank the Russian Army on both sides.

From our previous experience we could suppose that this offensive on our part would take the Russians quite by surprise and it appeared certain that we would have a great success over the forces that were opposing the 8th Army and the liberation of East Prussia would be the result. How the operations would afterwards develop I could naturally not foretell nor explain to the Chief of the General Staff. Even if the Russians were completely defeated, we were not strong enough to continue the operations against the fortified line Grodno-Kovno. On the other hand, we might hope after the Russians had been beaten by the envelopment of both their wings that we should succeed in advancing Southwards over the lines Grajevo-Augustovo, crossing the Bobr South of Augustovo and capturing the important fortress of Osoviec from the rear. The preliminary condition for the success of these operations was that we should hold the Southern frontier of East Prussia which till then was held only by the bulk of Zastrow's Corps and two Cavalry Divisions. Here the enemy had commenced the concentration of strong forces in preparation for his " gigantic " plan. In order to parry the expected attack we would have to send to the Southern Army all that the 9th Army could spare and bring them into action there.

I suggested to the Army Command that the newly formed Army should be placed under the command of H.I.H. the Crown Prince. Unfortunately my suggestions were not adopted. On the contrary the Commander-in-Chief in the East received the information that three of the new Corps and the 21st Army Corps that formed the 10th Army under the command of Field-Marshal von Eichhorn would be ready to be placed at his disposal in the first half of February for the operations that had been planned. One of the new Corps had been exchanged against the 21st Corps which was chiefly composed of Alsatian and Lorraine reserves, as it was desired to transfer this Corps from the Western to the Eastern front. I am unable to judge of the complaints that were raised in the West about the behaviour of the men of this Alsace-Lorraine Corps ; in the East they fought as splendidly as our other reserves.

General Ludendorff returned to Posen before the beginning of the battle and resumed his occupations as Chief of the General Staff.

It was naturally important to keep secret from the Russians the movement of the 9th Army towards the North[1] in order not to draw their attention on East Prussia too soon, and by so doing to render the surprise of the attack that was being prepared somewhat doubtful. The Commander-in-Chief in the East was therefore glad to agree to a proposal made by the Headquarters for the 9th Army to make an experiment with gas ammunition. The General Headquarters placed 18,000 shells at his disposal, a number that after the later experiences of the War would only raise a smile, but which, at the time we considered very important. General Schabel arrived with this ammunition from the General Headquarters. He was a great authority on artillery attacks on a large scale and in the use of gas shells.

The 9th Army proposed to make the attack at Bolymov, in order to improve the position at that place, that is to say the Army Command cherished very extensive optimistic hopes of the result, as General Schabel had represented the effects of the gas ammunition as very great indeed.

I arrived in Bolymov on the 31st, the day that had been chosen for the intended attack and watched the fight from the belfry of the Bolymov church. I was a little disappointed; from what General Schabel had told me I had expected much greater results from the employment of this ammunition in—as we then imagined—such large quantities. That the chief effect of the gas was destroyed by great cold was not known at that time. The

---

[1] 20th A.K. in the district South of Ortelsburg.
  1st Reserve Corps and 6th Cavalry—IV, round Willenberg.
  3rd Infantry—IV, round Neidenburg.
  1st Guard Reserve—IV, from Woyrsch's Army Division round Soldau.

tactical success, with the exception of considerable losses that the Russians sustained in killed and wounded was only a local improvement of our position ; this affair, however, drew the attention of the Russian front and Command on the 9th Army.

By the evening of the 6th February the 8th and 10th Armies stood ready for the attack.[1] The Commander-in-Chief in the East had removed his Headquarters to Insterburg.

The 20th Army Corps was still being detrained at Ortelsburg ; it was to defend the right flank of the Reserve Corps, to march on Myszciniec and to reconnoitre in the direction of the Narev. The Commander-in-Chief in the East also decided to carry on the task of defending the flank by an offensive action. The Command of the forces that were stationed between the Vistula and the Orzyc and the troops that were still to be concentrated there was undertaken by the Commander of the Guards Reserve Corps, General von Gallwitz.

On the 7th of February the Southern thrust troops under General von Lietzmann, the Commanding

---

[1] From the 10th Army there were in the front line :

    10th Landwehr Division, with its right wing North of Darkehmen connected with them the Landwehr Division of Königsberg formerly Chief Reserves).

    5th Guards Infantry Brigade, 1st Cavalry Division up to the fronts South of Memel. Behind them 38th Reserve Corps, 39th Reserve Corps, 21st A.C., all three North of the High road Instersburg—Gumbinnen.

    South of the 10th was the 8th Army ; 40th Reserve Corps and 2nd Infantry Division, between the frontier and the Spirding Lake ; behind them the 4th Cavalry Division.

    In the fortified positions of Lötzen, the 11th Landwehr Division and Landsturm.

    On the Angerapp from Angerburg to Darkehmen, 1st Landwehr Division and 3rd Reserve Division.

General of the 40th Reserve Corps, began the attack on Johannisburg and the Pissa sector to the South of it ; the 10th Army only began on the following day. The front of the 10th Army had orders, as soon as any signs of the enemy's retreat were observed at once to attack him and keep close at his heels.

It was no easy matter to keep to these dispositions. For many days there had been a real East Prussian snow storm. Everywhere the snow lay metre-high and the cutting East wind drifted it in places and formed high waves and walls ; to advance in close column was out of the question ; the artillery and the waggons remained sticking in the snow.

The Russians did not notice what we were planning. On the morning of the 7th and also on the 8th the reports that came in were : " Position of the enemy unchanged, everywhere he is seen shovelling the snow out of the trenches."

Already, in the afternoon of the 7th, General von Lietzmann had crossed the Pissa to the South of Johannesburg, on the 8th he took Johannesburg and having left troops to mask Osowiec forced his way during the next days as far as Raigorod. Here he met with strong Russian resistance, while, at the same time the enemy made an attack from Osowiec.

Thanks to the dashing but prudent orders given by General von Lietzmann the enemy was defeated at Raigorod and the attack from Osowiec was driven back.

The advance of the 10th Army that was begun early on the 8th met with but slight resistance from the Russians. They were taken quite by surprise and, as always in the case of an outflanking movement, they sought safety in a rapid retreat. The retirement of the Russian right wing was soon joined by the centre. The 8th Army then took up the pursuit and followed close at the retreating Russians' heels. In those days the chief enemy of the 10th Army was not the Russians but the weather; it was only with difficulty that the troops could work their way forwards. The columns of infantry were straggling, the bulk of the artillery and the vehicles remained sticking in the snow; only a few of the guns, to which twelve or eighteen horses were harnessed, and assisted by the infantry, were able to make their way forwards. Notwithstanding all these difficulties in the night from the 10th to the 11th the columns of the 10th Army were able to reach the high road to Kovno, not far from Wirbullen and Stallupönen.

Besides a great number of prisoners—troops from the Russian front that were retreating along the high roads and had been cut off—our troops captured large quantities of food and all sorts of provisions which were partly stored in depôts and partly still unloaded and standing in railway trains. Only this enabled the units of the 10th Army to advance as, in the condition in which the roads were, it would have been impossible to send supplies after the columns.

Although at the front the leaders and the soldiers, to the last man, did all they could the expected great success failed, owing to the physical impossibility of advancing quickly in such weather; large portions of the 10th Russian Army were able by retreating to get to a safe place before the circle could be closed around them.

On the 17th the pursuing 8th Army took Lyck,

which was defended by the 3rd Siberian Army. Unfortunately General von Lietzmann was unable to advance quick enough and the Corps escaped through Augustovo, and took refuge beyond the Bobr, while Lietzmann only reached Augustovo after hard fighting in the night from the 16th to the 17th.

The encircling columns of the 10th Army reached the approximate line Suwalki-Seiny on the 17th.

The Commander of the 10th Army still hoped, however, to be able to cut off considerable numbers of the enemy round Augustovo, and therefore issued orders for the further advance of the troops from the line Suwalki-Seiny.

In the meantime the weather had changed and the snow turned into impassable mud and floods.

The advance guard of the 21st Army Corps, which was advancing from Seiny in execution of the orders of the Commander of the 10th Army, who hoped to cut off the enemy near Augustovo, came upon strong Russian columns that were retreating along the high road which traversed the Augustovo forest. They were defeated and some prisoners taken.

The Commander of the 10th Army, realizing then that it had become impossible to overtake the enemy near Augustovo came to the bold decision of sending strong units of his left wing along the outskirts of the Augustovo forest as far as the district North-west of Grodno and to cut off the enemy when he issued from the forest, without paying any regard to the Grodno fortress.

The advance guard of the 8th Army which reached Augustovo had already received reports of the concentration of strong Russian forces around Lomza.

Two divisions were taken from the 8th Army, which had become congested as it advanced, and sent against Osowiec. One reason for this was that we wished to prevent enemy forces from issuing from Osowiec and another was that an attempt should be made to take it as the Commander-in-Chief in the East still entertained hopes that the 40th Reserve Corps, during the further development of the operations, would succeed in crossing the Upper Bobr and in opening the barrier fort from the rear.

The position of the troops of the 10th Army which were sent to cut off the Russian forces coming through the Augustovo forest West of Grodno was precarious, as on the one side the 20th Russian Army Corps, which found itself cut off in the forest, continued to make desperate efforts to break through, while from the other side the Russians in Grodno, where fresh troops had arrived, made constant sorties to assist their comrades who were shut in, to find a way out. But all the attacks from the East and the West were repulsed, and at last the Russian troops that were shut up in the forest had to surrender.

However gratifying it was to have defeated the 10th Russian Army, to have captured more than 100,000 prisoners, to have taken more than a hundred guns and quantities of provisions, we did not succeed in carrying out the operations to the desired end, nor in attaining the full strategic benefits we had looked for. General von Lietzmann was not able to cross the Bobr. The country was very difficult to negotiate ; the thaw, to which was now added constant rain, had turned the Bobr lowlands into a swamp ; on the high banks the 3rd Siberian

Corps was stationed in fortified positions, the troops said "in positions constructed of concrete." I did not believe in the "concrete," but my belief was not sufficient to bring the correctness of the soldiers' reports into doubt, and we were therefore obliged to give up the attempt to cross the Bobr. A year later, on the occasion of a reconnaissance, I was able to satisfy myself that I had been right, and that there were no traces of concrete to be seen.

Notwithstanding the participation of heavy artillery, the frontal attack on Osowiec had no success.

Already the day before, while the Commander-in-Chief in the East had still hopes of the progress of the operations on the other side of the Bobr, General Ludendorff had ordered the construction of a position in the rear on the lines East of Augustovo, East of Suwalki-Niemen.

The 10th Army now received an order to withdraw its right wing into this position. The left wing was allowed free action. At the same time it received orders to release forces that were urgently needed farther West.

Although by the offensive of our 8th and 10th Armies we had destroyed the first half of the "gigantic" plan of the Russian High Command, the outflanking of the German Army to the North in East Prussia, the execution of the second half, the advance of strong forces against the Southern frontier of East and West Prussia, began to make itself felt.

The 10th Army decided to withdraw its left wing only in the district of Seiny and North of that place, and to attack the Russians there if they attempted to pursue. The Army Command hoped to repeat the tactics of the winter battle on a smaller scale.

However the Russians only followed up hesitatingly and retired if we attempted to attack. The Army Command therefore decided to give up the idea of attacking and withdraw the left wing to the line Kalwaja-Majampol-Pilwiszki. During March the Russians attacked these positions but were repulsed with ease.

At the beginning of the attack of the 40th Reserve Corps, the 20th Army Corps and the 37th Infantry Division went by way of Myszeziniec, with the 41st Infantry Division by way of Kolno, towards Lomza, in order to cover the flank of General Lietzmann's attack. The Corps came upon strong enemy forces, and its strength only sufficed to cover the flank Eastwards as far as Stawiszki.

In the space between Stawiszki and the Bobr the 3rd Reserve Division and the 5th Infantry Brigade were now pushed in.

The above-mentioned units arrived just in time to meet an attack of the Russian Guards Corps and the 5th Army Corps from Lomza. A desperate struggle ensued ; the Russians attacked bravely regardless of losses, and the 3rd Reverve Division was only able to maintain its position with the greatest difficulty. Only in the beginning of March was it possible to send the 1st Landwehr Division there and thus to give to that front the necessary strength and density.

Similar furious attacks were made on the line Ostrolenke-Novgorod against the 37th Infantry Division which was holding the line South of Myszeziniec between the Orzic and the Pissa.

The Commander-in-Chief in the East found

himself obliged to send more and more troops to its assistance,[1] the immeasurable extent of wood and bogland unfortunately obliged him to do so.

Fighting continued here during the whole of March, but the German troops were able to hold out.

In the middle of February the Russians had received reinforcements to the West of Orzic, opposite the Gallwitz sector, and they began to advance towards Mlawa.

When the reinforcements from the 9th Army had arrived, General von der Gallwitz decided to anticipate the Russian attack, and to make a thrust into their midst.

The attack that was begun on the 22nd February by the 1st Reserve Corps, the 3rd Division Landwehr and Landsturm, under General von Morgen, progressed at first successfully. General von Förster's Division even succeeded in taking Prasznysz, but then a reaction set in ; one of the Landwehr Brigades failed us. Strong Russian forces pressed forward from the South on Prasznysz and tried to outflank us from the Orzic.

With their flank menaced the 1st Reserve Corps and the 3rd Division had to give up Prasnysz and to retreat. Further South, where the frontier positions were still being constructed, General von Ludendorff stopped the troops. In the first week of March the Russians made embittered attacks on our positions between Mlawa and the Orzic, but they were all repulsed.

---

[1] 2nd I = .
  75th Reserves = IV.
  10th Landwehr = IV.
  4th Cavalry = IV.
  and later, 76th Reserves = IV.

After the arrival of the reinforcements, General von der Gallwitz began an offensive advance on the 8th of March, on both sides of the Orzic ; by the 12th, he had succeeded in driving the enemy back to the North of Prasnysz. Here again there were strong Russian counter attacks which although they were unsuccessful, brought our advance to a standstill.

The fighting continued till the end of March and then grew gradually weaker.

By April the Russian attacks had been repulsed along the whole of the Prussian Southern front, and thus the second part of the Grand Duke Nicolai Nicolaievich's " gigantic " plan was finished with.

Our Austro-Hungarian Ally did not succeed in carrying out his plans so successfully. The offensive for the relief of Przemysl had to be stopped as soon as the Russians began a counter attack. The fate of Przemysl was sealed.

From the middle of February small fights began in the corner of East Prussia, North of the Memel. The Russians had still frontier guard detachments on German territory North-east of Tilsit.

The Commander-in-Chief in the East naturally desired to clear this corner of German ground from the enemy. General von Pappritz, the Governor of Königsberg was given the order to do it ; his Chief of Staff was Colonel Nehbel. He had only at his disposal the Landsturm that served as frontier guards and the little artillery from Königsberg. Nevertheless the offensive succeeded. By February the enemy was driven across the frontier and Tauroggen was taken.

The satisfaction we felt at having freed the whole of German territory from the enemy was of short duration.

On the 17th of March, Memel was attacked by a small body of frontier guards and territorials, under the command of General Potapov. The attack took us by surprise; reports had been received of the concentration of Russian troops opposite Tauroggen and Memel, but they were not considered of much importance; it must not be forgotten that alarming reports of concentrations of troops and some sort of enemy attack were received in dozens every day, and it was not necessary to give credence to every report that came in.

More accurate news of the entry of the Russians into Memel came from the telephone girl of the Memel Post Office, Fräulein Röstel. She displayed more energy than her male colleagues and spoke with me until the Post Office was occupied by the Russians. Our conversation was closed on her side with the words: "They are just coming up the stairs."

At the same time that Memel was surprised, the Russians also attacked Tauroggen and General von Pappritz was forced to give it up as he required all his weak forces against Memel and the enemy who was there. The Commander-in-Chief in the East had no sort of reserves at his disposal to send as reinforcements to General von Pappritz. The Deputy General Command of the II Army Corps in Stettin sent us two *Ersatz* Battalions.

We had luck: the Russians themselves were not strong. They evacuated Memel when Pappritz approached the town and we succeeded in recapturing 3,000 prisoners they were carrying off.

Pappritz then turned against the enemy at Tau-roggen, drove him over the frontier and retook Tauroggen on the 29th of March.

Something had to be done to prevent such a surprise being repeated. The 6th Cavalry Division which for the time was not necessary in Gallwitz's front was transferred to the district East of Memel.

In the middle of April things calmed down on the Eastern front.

CHAPTER IX

GORLICE

In the meantime the conditions had not developed in a very satisfactory manner in the Southern theatre of war.

As has already been mentioned, the attack on the Carpathian front, that General von Conrad had decided to make, had not been successful. At the very commencement it met with a Russian counter offensive and was stopped. The more the Russian High Command became convinced that their plans against East Prussia and the German Army would not be successful the stronger their attacks became against the Austro-Hungarian troops. This Spring they wanted to bring about a decisive battle regardless of what it might cost them in men.

There were fierce and bloody battles between the Carpathian ridges in the midst of snow and ice, which although they caused the Russians unheard of losses, drove our Allies slowly back. The position of the Austro-Hungarian Army became very critical. If the Russians had succeeded in breaking through the line and passing over the Carpathians into the plains of Hungary, the Dual-Monarchy would be broken up. Germany was obliged to do something energetic to support her Allies.

Captain von Fleischmann, the Austro-Hungarian liaison officer, told us every day in the office of the

Headquarters' Staff when he made his report that the situation was very grave and each day he repeated it with more and more emphasis. The Commander-in-Chief in the East was of the same opinion and he represented this matter to the General Headquarters. From his own forces the Commander-in-Chief in the East sent a Division acting as Reserves to the 9th Army. It reached the Carpathians in the middle of April at a very critical moment, just when Boroevic's Army was beginning to waver. The General Headquarters approved of the dispatch of this Division (25th Reserve Division) and they ordered two other Divisions to be sent as reinforcements to the Carpathian front, and the General Command, 38th Reserve Corps, was to be sent too. General von der Marwitz was appointed as Commander of this newly formed Beskiden Corps by order of the Chief High Command. The Commander-in-Chief in the East gave up these four Divisions and also a newly formed Division.

The General Headquarters had begun, shortly before this time, to take from each of the Divisions on the Western front one infantry regiment and to form new Divisions out of the regiments obtained in this way. They gained in this way a large number of tactical units. It was possible in a war of positions for each Division to give up three battalions as new positions continued to be built. This inspired idea originated with General von Wrisberg, the Departmental Director in the War Office. Later on, before the end of the War, a dispute arose between the different military authorities as to whether it was more practical to keep the Divisions at nine battalions or to raise them to twelve battalions as before. The smaller Divisions had the advantage of being easier to operate with, but the disadvantage for some tasks of being too weak in infantry. For Germany no decision could be arrived at on this disputed question, as by the fatal Resolution of Versailles our fine army was doomed to dissolution, and all such controversial questions that arose out of the experiences of the War have now only an academic interest for us.

About this time we, in the East, began also to reform our Divisions in this manner.

The German reinforcements that were sent to the Carpathians were unable to produce a sudden change ; they were only able to hold the position. But it was not only in the Carpathians but on all the fronts that the position of the Allied Monarchies became more and more serious.

The Serbian Army began to move and the chief thing was that it became more certain every week that Italy would openly join the Alliance against us. I leave it an open question if it would have been possible by sacrifices made by Austro-Hungary and by adroit negotiations made by the Central Powers, to have persuaded Italy to maintain her neutrality—in any case the Austrian High Command found himself obliged to reinforce his garrisons along the Italian frontier if she did not wish to be taken quite by surprise from a military standpoint if Italy joined the War. She was obliged to take these reinforcements from the Russian front which was already weak.

If the German General Headquarters had followed the suggestion of the Commander-in-Chief in the East and had sent to the East, in the late Autumn of 1914, the reinforcements that were necessary, in order to defeat decisively the main Russian forces which were wedged in between a bend of the Vistula, all these difficulties would have been avoided. Thus lost opportunities are a phenomenon of this War that we shall often have to notice. The right thing is suggested at the right moment, when success can be achieved with but a comparatively small employment of force, but the suggestion is set aside ; then enemy movements take place that oblige the General Headquarters to send more reinforcements than had previously been asked for : with only this difference, that the forces now no longer serve to gain a decisive victory but only to retrieve a misfortune that had occurred.

Already some time previously General von Conrad had suggested to General von Falkenhayn, in a personal conversation he had had with him, the idea of breaking through the Russian front at Gorlice, to roll up the Russian forces that were stationed before the Carpathian passes. The plan was the only one that at the time offered any hope of clearing the Carpathian front in time ; naturally it was desirable to make the thrust at one of the wings and to outflank the Russian Army in this way. The outflanking attack is always the most effective. It was however impossible to begin the operations against the Russian wing in the Bukowina. The Austro-Hungarian railways were so untrustworthy that it was quite out of the question to attempt sending large transports of troops quickly by them.

It was quite possible to attack the Russian North wing by an outflanking movement, to take Kovno and to make a strong thrust in the direction of Kovno-Vilna. The plan offered good prospects of success. This operation would however have taken a long time before its effects could have been felt on the Russian left wing in the Carpathians. Therefore to break through the Russian line at Gorlice was a much better idea. General von Falkenhayn had acknowledged this to General von Conrad at a consultation they had had together in the Hotel Adlon in Berlin, but he had refused to place at his disposal the forces necessary for the execution of this plan.

Now, however, General von Falkenhayn realized that something had to be done to prevent a complete breakdown of the Austro-Hungarian front in the Carpathians. The number of German troops that General von Conrad would have required for this defensive action was nearly as large as would have been required if the offensive solution of the position had been adopted. General von Falkenhayn reverted to General von Conrad's plan of breaking through at Gorlice.

In his book General von Falkenhayn is silent about the inventor of the idea.

During the campaign we have often had occasion to complain of the deficiencies of the Austro-Hungarian Army ; we ought therefore all the more to acknowledge the help that we received from our Ally. The ideas of the Chief of the Austrian General Staff were good—at least as far as they became known to me—they were all good, and this cannot always be said of the ideas of our own Commander-in-Chief. The misfortune of that man of genius was that he had not the proper instrument by which he could transform his ideas into facts. The troops failed, while with us, on the contrary, whether they were well or badly led, they never failed until the Summer of 1918.

The decision of the General Headquarters at last to try to obtain a decisive result in the East must be approved of, as it was to be expected that this attack on the Russians would produce attacks in the West to relieve the pressure there. The great French attack in Champagne in February and March had indeed been repulsed, but it had cost us dearly. It was necessary to be prepared to meet similar attempts to break through that might be made on a large scale.

The Command of the 11th Army that was appointed to effect the break-through was given to General von Mackensen, and the Chief of his Staff was Colonel von Seeckt ; the place of General von Mackensen was taken by Field-Marshal Prince Leopold of Bavaria who had been waiting impatiently at home for an appointment at the front, and he willingly placed himself under Field-Marshal von Hindenburg though Hindenburg was junior to him in the service.

In order to mask the preparations that were being made for the attack on Gorlice, and to draw the attention of the enemy off this point, the Commander-in-Chief in the East was ordered to make demonstrations on his front so as to keep as many enemy forces as possible there and to draw them upon himself.

In accordance with the instructions received from the General Headquarters, the Commander-in-Chief in the East decided to attack the enemy at three different places. A gas attack was to be made by the 9th Army, the 10th Army was to make a local attack at Suwalki in order to improve its positions, and lastly we planned a greater invasion of Northern Lithunia and Courland. While the two first attacks were of only local importance, we expected that the last one would have great results, as the Russians would be obliged to take measures on a large scale to repel it.

For the execution of the gas attack one of the newly formed Gas Battalions had been sent us some time before ; by reconnoitring, a place in the neighbourhood of Skierniwice had been found that was favourable for such an attack, and the cylinders for the emission of the gas had been dug into the ground at that place. The preparations had all been made at that time and the 9th Army was only waiting for a favourable wind.

The idea of the emission of gases cannot be considered as a happy one ; there were but few places on the front that were suitable for it ; the digging in of the apparatus was very complicated, and at any moment there was the danger of the enemy noticing the work of digging in and by strong artillery fire destroying the apparatus and the gas would then stream out in our own trenches. Besides this the weather conditions of our theatre of war were very unfavourable for such gas emissions ; in the East we required a West wind—in the West an East wind, but as on our front the wind was mostly contrary, the employment of this invention was rendered still more difficult. The hopes on the German side that our opponents would not be able to imitate this process was also not realized. Later I was able to ask the clever inventor of our gas substance, the Geheimrat Haber, how he had come upon such an unfortunate process. He explained to me that he had foreseen all these defects and from the first he had considered it would have been better not to emit the gas, but to use it in the form of gas shells ; but at the beginning he was not given space enough to make this ammunition. It was only for this reason that he had thought of emitting it from cylinders.

It is very much to be regretted that this idea of Geheimrat Haber was not carried out from the beginning. If you take for granted that from the first he had come upon somebody with the necessary understanding and that a large quantity of ammunition filled with gas substance had been secretly prepared ; that at some great fight to break through the line in the West it had suddenly been employed—at a time when the enemy still knew nothing of the danger of gas attacks and gas-masks had not been introduced—then it is scarcely possible to imagine the success it would have had.

On the 2nd of May, the wind being favourable, the 9th Army made an attack with gas. We heard later that its success in the Russian positions was very great ; unfortunately this was not realized by our troops. The soldiers believed that the adversary would be entirely destroyed after the gas cloud had passed over their positions ; when our infantry advanced and were shot at from several places, it was thought that the gas attack had not succeeded and the advance was given up. A later attempt with gas also made by the 9th Army was likewise not calculated to increase the confidence of the troops. This time gas had only just been emitted when the wind veered round and a part of the gas cloud was blown back into our own trenches and we had considerable losses. The troops in the East were only provided with gas-masks much later than the Western Army, as was always the case under all circumstances.

The attack made by the 10th Army had the desired tactical success—a slight improvement of the position.   Further attempts of the 9th and 10th Armies succeeded in attracting the attention of the Russians to them, but they did not succeed, however, in fulfilling the commission that the General Headquarters had given to the Commander-in-Chief in the East of obliging the Russians to concentrate large forces on that front.   This commission we were only able to carry out by our attacks on North Lithuania and Courland.

The direct impulse to this attack was given by the General Headquarters.   In the second half of March they inquired of the Commander-in-Chief in the East if he considered a cavalry raid from his left wing, in the direction of Kovno perhaps, as possible.   As he answered in the affirmative, the General Headquarters sent him two Cavalry Divisions from the West for the execution of this raid. They arrived about the middle of April.

On the 26th of April we were ready for the undertaking.[1]

On the 27th of April, General von Lauenstein began to advance with these units from the line Jurborg-Memel, for the attack on Courland.   He drove the weaker Russian forces back and reached Schaulen in a single spurt.   The Russians sent reinforcements and fighting began on the line from the

---

[1] There were stationed :

    Bavarian Cavalry Division and 3rd Cavalry Division South of Furborg.
      Behind them, 36th Reserve Division.
    78th Reserve Division on the Tauroggen high road.
    6th Cavalry Division and 3rd Reserve Division around Memel.

river Dubissa-Schaulen-Mosheiki that obliged us also to send reinforcements. From them and Lauenstein's original detachment the Niemen Army, under the command of General von Below, was formed later. In place of General von Below, General von Scholtz undertook the command of the 8th Army.

In the severe fighting that took place in the months of May and June we were able to maintain our positions on the Dubissa and our left wing was able to hold the Windau. Owing to Russian superior forces we were obliged to give up Schaulen.

On our extreme left wing the small fortress of Libau was taken by a surprise attack on the 7th of May. The 3rd Cavalry Brigade, as well as a small party of Landsturm and Artillery from Königsberg took part in this lucky undertaking. The attack was led by Colonel von der Schulenburg and a very capable officer of the General Staff, Captain von Willisen, who was afterwards often mentioned in despatches.

On the 2nd of May, the 11th German Army and the 4th Austro-Hungarian Army, under the command of General von Mackensen, took Tarnow, the first Russian position near Gorlice. In the following days Mackensen stormed the second and third lines and forced the whole of the Russian front in the Carpathians to retire.

On the 15th of May the 11th Army reached the San.

In the beginning of June Przemysl was taken.

After a short pause on the San the attack was continued and on the 22nd of June Lemberg fell.

Rawaruska was stormed and the Russians were driven back towards the Bug.

H

At each of these stages Falkenhayn wanted to stop the advance and finish the operation. Each time it was only thanks to Conrad's insistence that he was induced to allow the advance to be continued.

On our front the Russian defeat made itself felt also, as everywhere the Russians were bringing up forces in order to dispatch them to the South.

The Commander-in-Chief in the East was not strong enough to prevent it ; all he could do was to bring up forces too, and to hold them in readiness for a new operation. The question was only where they could best be employed.

Our discussions at Headquarters on this subject often became very lively. From the beginning I supported the opinion that we had now perhaps for the last time the possibility of dealing the Russian Army an overwhelming blow. General von Mackensen's offensive would gradually wear itself out as he had always to make frontal attacks ; the continuation of this advance could never result in an overwhelming blow for the Russian Army. The only enemy wing which was still open to our attacks on the whole of the Continent was the right Russian wing that lay opposite the Army of the Commander-in-Chief in the East. Against this wing a large outflanking operation ought to be made to the North or the North-east, so that the middle of the Russian line which was still before Warsaw on the Ravka and the Bzura would not be able to escape the blow by retiring, but that it would be cut off.

I therefore supported the opinion that all the forces that the Commander-in-Chief in the East could spare from the sphere under his orders, as well as all the troops that could be obtained from the General Headquarters, should be brought into action in the left wing of the 10th Army. Kovno should be taken in the shortest time possible and the offensive attack be carried over Vilna to the rear of the chief Russian forces.

It is still my opinion that if these operations had been carried out, the results would have been most satisfactory and would have led to the complete defeat of the Russian Army.

Major von Bockelberg, who enjoyed the special confidence of General Ludendorff, from having worked together with him for many years in the Second Division of the Great General Staff, pleaded, of course not in official reports, which he had no right to make, but in private conversations, for an offensive across the Bobr on both sides of Osowice. I considered an offensive across the swampy lowlands of the Bobr, where we would be quite unable to assist the attacks of our infantry with the bulk of our artillery was wrong, and that such an attempt would be doomed to failure from the very beginning. His chief objection to my plan was that the capture of Kovno would take too much time. Later events proved that I was right ; in August we took Kovno, if not in opposition to the wishes of the General Headquarters, at least without much support from them, in ten days. If the plan that I proposed had been carried out, this time might even have been shortened by a few days.

General Ludendorff was of my opinion.

We were all of the opinion that an offensive against the sector of the front West of Lomza would be useless. By such an attack we would naturally be able to force the Russians to give up their positions in the centre and to evacuate Warsaw ; but it would never bring about a decisive defeat. If we made the attack so far to the West, the Russians could easily draw in the outer curve of their front to form a straight line and we would soon be doing exactly what Mackensen was doing in the South : making a frontal advance as the enemy retired.

The preparations for the advance on Kovno and beyond were begun. The Orders, as far as the replacement of troops in the area that was under the command of the Commander-in Chief in the East is concerned, were already planned out, when Field-Marshal von Hindenburg and General Ludendorff were ordered by telegraph to make a report to H.M. the Kaiser in Pösen on the 1st of July.

General Ludendorff and I did not doubt that His Majesty would approve of the plan to make an attack on Kovno ; General Ludendorff arranged with me that immediately after the audience he would ring me up and that then I was to send out the orders that were already prepared.

I waited in vain for the telephone call.

It was only in the afternoon that I received instructions to stop everything ; it turned out otherwise than we had expected. His Majesty while in Pösen had approved of General von Falkenhayn's plan, by which General von Gallwitz was to break through the Russian front opposite his positions, and make an attack towards the Narev. By this move, in my opinion, the last possibility of making a destructive attack on the Russian Army was lost. This Gallwitz attack might be as successful as it could be, but it could only result in the Russians having to give up Warsaw and their salient positions in Poland.

The 12th Army[1]—the former Gallwitz detachment—was quite ready on the 13th of July for the attack on Prasznicz and the enemy positions on both sides of that place.

Thanks to the examplary arrangements of the High Command of the Army, the attack succeeded perfectly. The Army broke through the Russian positions and reached the Narev on the 17th. Here there was naturally a certain pause. Pultusk and Rozan were taken on the 23rd of July. Ostrolenka on the 4th of August and the river was crossed on a broad front. The right wing turned towards Novo-Georgievsk and Zegrze.

The 8th Army had likewise begun to advance and after severe fighting had also reached the Narev, where it met with stubborn resistance from the Russians. The object of this fierce resistance of the 12th and 8th Armies was naturally only to give the Russian troops time to retire from the Warsaw salient.

As we had expected, as soon as the Russian High Command realized that the break through of the 12th Army was not to be resisted, it had given orders for the general retreat out of Poland.

The Russians that were stationed opposite the Woyrsch Detachments and the 9th Army were already considerably weakened by the forces that they had had to send to the South. Both Armies now began to attack. The Woyrsch Detachment

---

[1] 1st A.C. (2nd and 37th I.D.).
   12th A.C. (3rd and 26th I. = and 4th Guard Reserve Division).
   17th A.C. (35th and 36th I. = and 1st Guard Reserve Division).
   11th A.C. (38th I. = and = IV Wernitz).
   17th Reserve Corps (Landwehr Division von Brenghel and 14th Landwehr = IV).
   Dickhut's Corps.

met strong rear-guard detachments on the Ilshanke and at Radom which it defeated and drove beyond the Vistula. To the North of the Pilica and with the 9th Army there was no heavy fighting. The Russians gave up the land West of the Vistula and hurried back to Warsaw.

In the meantime about the middle of July the Niemen Army on the left wing of the forces that had been placed under the command of the Commander-in-Chief of the East, had again begun an offensive and it was advancing victoriously.

The 10th Army also pressed forwards on Kovno and drove the Russians behind the Liesna segment.

About this time General Ludendorff was again summoned to the General Headquarters. He pointed out that the offensive of General Gallwitz had only led to the results that the Commander-in-Chief in the East had foretold, and that to continue this offensive would not lead to any better results than it had done already. He repeated the suggestion of taking all the available troops from the Woyrsch Army Detachment, from the 12th and 8th Armies, to transport them to the 10th Army, to take Kovno and then make an attack on Vilna with all these forces.

These operations might even yet have had great success. Whether it would still have been possible to inflict on the Russians an overwhelming defeat, that is a defeat which would have caused the Tzar to turn his thoughts towards peace, must remain an open question.

The General Headquarters again rejected these suggestions and ordered the continuation of the offensive in the direction already begun. Nevertheless the Commander-in-Chief in the East held fast to his idea of taking Kovno and of sending the left wing of the troops under his command as far forward as possible. The General Headquarters reinforced the 12th and 8th Armies by sending to each of them a Division from the West ; the Commander-in-Chief in the East sent to the 12th Army two more Divisions from the 9th Army.

The Russian High Command had apparently 1812 in their mind during this retreat ; they not only destroyed all communications, but they also burned towns and villages and drove the people and cattle away towards the East with the retreating army. For some unaccountable reason, they seemed to believe that in this way they would cause us more than temporary difficulties, otherwise their conduct would have only been useless cruelty towards their own people. It is a strange thing that even now comparisons with 1812 often appear in German periodicals and newspapers. The people who write them do not realize that the difficulties that Napoleon had at that time in his campaigns have been overcome by modern means of communications and conveyance. If Napoleon had had railways, telephones, motors, the telegraph and airmen he would be in Moscow to-day.

With the exception of temporary difficulties with regard to quarters, the Russian destructions were in many ways an advantage for us. Let us take for example, the burning of Brest-Litovsk, where afterwards the Commander-in-Chief in the East had his Headquarters for nearly two years : although it was burnt down we were able to find quarters there, while the 80,000 inhabitants, for whom we should have had to provide, were not there. For the risks of espionage and other dangers it was also quite convenient for us that the town was entirely evacuated.

After having received the above mentioned reinforcements the 12th Army recommenced its advance. The forces under Mackensen also pressed forward from the South. The General Headquarters tried to outflank various portions of the Russian front, but in general without success, as the Commander-in-Chief in the East had foreseen.

By the end of July Cholm and Lublin were taken. The Woyrsch Detachment and the Kövesz Group stormed the bridgehead at Ivangorod and at the end of July Woyrsch crossed the Vistula North of Ivangorod in the very sight of the Russians. This crossing was a bold military exploit which however did not lead to any great success ; on the contrary, the units that had crossed the river were fiercely attacked by the Russians and found themselves in a difficult position for a time.

Before the advance of the 9th Army the Russians evacuated the outposts of Warsaw and the town itself at the beginning of August. On the 5th of August the 9th Army occupied Warsaw.

On that same day the Woyrsch Army Detachment and the 9th Army were removed out of the sphere under the command of the Commander-in-Chief in the East and were placed under the immediate control of the General Headquarters as the Army Group of Prince Leopold of Bavaria. A tactical reason for this new ruling of the spheres of command was unknown to me at the time and I was never able afterwards to find out the reasons that had prompted it. On the contrary, when difficulties occurred on the Eastern front in 1916, not only were these units again put under the Commander-in-Chief of the East but the sphere of his authority was extended, after some opposition by the Austro-Hungarian High Command, as far as the Carpathians. I can therefore only suppose that these measures were taken by the General Headquarters owing to the dissensions that existed between them and the Commander-in-Chief in the East.

After the occupation of Warsaw the whole of the Army Group of Prince Leopold of Bavaria crossed the Vistula between Ivangorod and Warsaw and continued the pursuit of the Russians towards the Bug, North of Brest Litovsk, while the Mackensen Army Group remained quartered at Brest-Litovsk.

After crossing the Narev the 12th Army took a Southern direction in the hope of being able to cut off some Russian units near Warsaw. This hope proved vain as the Commander-in-Chief in the East and General Gallwitz had foretold it would, and they also turned Eastwards, while the 8th Army after taking Ostrolenka marched on Lomza.

General von Beseler, the conqueror of Antwerp, was commissioned to invest and take as quickly as possible Novo-Georgievsk. He was assisted by his very able Chief of Staff, General von Sauberzweig.

Owing to excellent leadership and the energetic attacks of the besieging army, which consisted entirely of Landwehr and Landsturm troops, the fortress fell on the 19th of August.

The Russian High Command had doubtless over-estimated the value of the ring of frontier fortresses when they decided to continue the defence of Novo-Georgievsk and to leave a garrison of 80,000 men there. The bitter experiences they had had with Novo-Georgievsk and Kovno were probably the causes that afterwards made them decide not to attempt the defence of the strong fortress of Brest-Litovsk.

Notwithstanding all the difficulties of the task, in the beginning of August the Commander-in-Chief in the East decided to take Kovno. Two batteries of 42-cm. guns was all the heavy artillery he had at his disposal, as the chief part of our heavy artillery had to be brought into action against Novo-Georgievsk. The General Headquarters gave us no ammunition ; but owing to economy General Ludendorff had a small stock of ammunition, which he placed at the disposal of the 10th Army.

It was only by thinning the line of its front in other parts and by weakening it in an almost unpermissible manner, that the 10th Army could obtain the necessary number of troops for the attack. However the troops had such a strong feeling of superiority over the Russians that the leaders, General von Eichhorn and his Chief of Staff, Colonel Helt, as well as General Lietzmann, the leader of the assaulting troops, were quite willing to take the risks upon themselves.

On the 6th of August the infantry was pushed forward nearer to the fortress, on the 8th the artillery opened fire. Although the Russians defended themselves fiercely, by the 15th General Lietzmann had driven them behind the line of forts ; on the 16th, a company, taking them by surprise, broke in from the banks of the Niemen. The result of the fighting that followed was that the line of forts was taken and on the 17th General Lietzmann crossed the Niemen and took the town and the Eastern forts. After the fall of the Western line of forts the Russians gave up all attempts at resistance, and hurriedly retreated on Vilna. The bridges across the Niemen, especially the railway bridge—the loss of which was most painful to us—were naturally blown up. On the other hand the railway tunnel had only been slightly injured, and with the help of the material we had captured, we were soon able to establish communications with Vilna by means of trolleys, which was of great importance for the continuation of our operations.

After the fall of Kovno, General von Eichhorn pushed the troops that were on his left wing across the Niemen and sent them along the railway line towards Vilna. It was characteristic of the conditions of the means of communication in Tzarish Russia that there was no metalled road, not even a proper high road between Vilna, the chief town of the Vilna Government, the residence of the Governor, and the important garrison and industrial town of Kovno.

General von Eichhorn sent the right wing of his Army, under General von Hutier, to continue the advance in the direction of Olita. Weaker units were sent through the Augustov forest towards Grodno. They were in touch with the left wing of the 8th Army which, after the fall of Osoviec, was advancing on Grodno.

General von Hutier drove the Russian rear-guard which fought fiercely into the wooded country towards the Niemen, and forced them over it ; he reached Olita on the 26th of August, crossed the Niemen at the end of August and pressed on to Vilna along the railway. The Russian resistance became stronger here. Nevertheless Hutier's advance made itself felt Southwards and the Russians evacuated Grodno.

The left wing of the 8th Army took the South-west front on the 1st of September, and after severe street fighting the town was taken on the 2nd of September.

East of Grodno we met with strong opposition on Lake Osicry. To the right of the 8th Army, the 12th Army had reached the Svisloez by this time, and the Army Group of Prince Leopold of Bavaria had crossed the Bialovicz forest.

On the extreme left wing of the Niemen Army the position was now as follows : General von Below had been able to hold the line that had been reached in June : the Dubissa as far South as Schaulen ; the Wenta and the Windau as far North as Hasenpot. In the beginning of July the reinforcements sent him by the Commander-in-Chief in the East and which have already been mentioned, began to arrive. With their arrival General von Below received an order to recommence the advance, and to begin by cutting off the enemy that was stationed at Schaulen.

General von Below collected together the 1st Reserve Corps and formed a strong attacking force out of his left wing, leaving the rest of the front quite thinly manned and began operations about the middle of July. The strong left wing was to advance in the direction of Mitau, and to envelop the enemy stationed at Schaulen from the North, while the 1st Reserve Corps advanced to the South.

The Russians were again taken by surprise by our offensive. As always they defended themselves energetically and one of their attacks on our 6th Reserve Division in the direction of Okmiany forced this Division to retire towards the West. However the pressure from the South soon obliged the Russians to desist from their attack on the 6th Reserve Division and in their turn they had to retire.

On the 17th the left wing defeated the Russians at Autz, and after several days' fighting at Schaulen the whole of the Russian 5th Army was driven back in the direction of Ponieviez. Ponieviez was taken on the 29th of July and Mitau on the 1st of August. Even the weak right wing crossed the Dubissa and one detachment pushed on against Kovno.

To the South of Riga the Russians halted at a large fortified bridgehead. On the other hand we succeeded in driving the Russians to the North bank of the river between Üxküll and Friedrichstadt. With this the attacking power of the Niemen Army was brought to an end. For its weak forces it occupied a very large space, and reinforcements were difficult to send owing to the conditions of the roads ; besides which the Commander-in-Chief in the East had been obliged to send the larger number of his columns to Gallwitz's 12th Army. However, this successful advance of the Niemen Army not-withstanding its weak forces, only proves that the Russians would not have been able to repulse an advance made by the forces of the Commander-in-Chief of the East and the attack ordered by the General Headquarters in the direction of Kovno-Vilna, supported on the left wing by the advance of the Niemen Army.

It was only in the middle of August that the Commander-in-Chief in the East was permitted to continue his offensive in the direction of Vilna. This was naturally too late for him to be able to obtain any decided advantage over the Russian Army ; consequently it became only a question of local successes. The General Headquarters permitted the blockading troops from Novo-Georgievsk and some Divisions of the Reserves that had been taken from the 8th and 12th Armies to be sent to the 10th Army. The bulk of the troops that could be released from the Armies that were now being squeezed together during the further advance, was destined for the West and for the Serbian theatre of war.

In the meantime halfway between Kovno and Vilna the 10th Army had had fierce fighting. The Russian High Command had sent to the North part of the troops that were retreating from Poland. The enemy forces that were here facing the left wing of the 10th Army, though part of a connected line towards the North, was weak and it was easy to break through their line. The chief necessity for a further advance of the left wing in the direction of Vilna-Minsk was to cut the railway lines from Dorinsk and Molodeczno that were on the flanks and the rear of the attacking forces.

The Niemen Army therefore received the order to advance on Dvinsk as soon as the 10th Army renewed the attack ; the strong cavalry of the 10th Army was told to go towards the railway line near Polozk and specially to the Molodeczno junction.

The transport of reinforcements took an endlessly long time. The railway, Wirballen-Kovno, was in a far from efficient condition and required first to be put in order, the roads were bad and the horses were tired and worn out.

The renewed attack could only begin on the 9th of September.

General von Eichhorn and Colonel Hell, his Chief of Staff, were very hopeful and they also infected General Ludendorff with their optimistic anticipations. The line was broken through quite successfully, the cavalry reached the railway line, the 1st Cavalry Division went even as far as Smorgon; the Russians were obliged to give up Vilna, but then the advance stopped; it had been commenced too late. At that time the Russian retreat from Poland was so far successful that the Russians could simply wheel in Divisions from their fronts that lay farther to the South.

The 1st Cavalry Division fought like heroes in a battle they had at Smorgon. They were attacked by superior Russian forces but they thought they would be able to hold Smorgon and that they must hold it until the infantry came up; but owing to the bad roads it arrived too late, and after having sustained heavy losses the Division was obliged to evacuate Smorgon.

The Russian High Command also brought up strong forces by rail to the country round Dvinsk. The Niemen Army was unable to take Dvinsk. The attack was brought to a standstill here also.

Now the Russians began attacks on the whole front of the 10th Army and on the right wing of the Niemen Army. Their attacks were everywhere repulsed; our troops succeeded in a few places in taking some more ground.

General Ludendorff realized that the operations must be stopped; it was now impossible to attain a success. The entire German offensive was suspended, the left wing of the 10th Army was drawn back, and in connexion with the Army Group of Prince Leopold, who in his advance Northwards had reached Minsk-Baronovice. The winter positions were taken up on the line Beresina-Krevo-Lake Norocz-Lake Drysviaty-Novo-Alexandrovsk-Dvina. For a short time fighting continued near Lake

Norocz and more especially before Dvinsk where the 1st Reserve Corps still continued to hope to be able to capture the bridgehead of Dvinsk; but gradually quiet settled down on the whole front.

The High Command of the Austro-Hungarian Army felt very justly that it was inconvenient that the Russian lines should be less than two days' march to the East and North-east of such an important railway junction as Lemberg. General von Conrad had therefore planned an attack from the country round Homel on the gap that really existed in Volhynia between the Southern and South-western Russian fronts, in order to press upon the North wing of the Russian South-west front and in consequence of this pressure to free the rest of Galicia from the Russians.

The German General Headquarters had approved of the Austrian Commander-in-Chief's plan and after the fall of Brest-Litovsk at the end of August they had consented to the withdrawal from the Mackensen Army Group of the 4th and 1st Austro-Hungarian Armies, which had been sent to assist in that operation. Unfortunately, in this undertaking General von Conrad had his usual want of success. The idea was right, but the instrument failed him. The attack was forced back by a Russian counter attack.

The campaign of 1915 was ended for the Commander-in-Chief in the East when the permanent positions were taken up.

The Entente's plan by a simultaneous attack of the Russian masses on Prussia and the Carpathians to bring the War to an end had failed. The Russians had been beaten along the whole front and they had sustained losses from which they were unable to recover. But it had not been possible to defeat the Russians so completely as to compel them to sue for peace. And yet (I wish again to emphasize this fact) the possibility of doing so had been there. If our General Headquarters had decided in July, 1915, to transfer all the available forces to the 10th Army, to take Kovno and to make a strong attack in the direction of Vilna-Minsk, at a time when the Russian troops were still in Poland to the West of Warsaw, the defeat of the Russians must have been a decisive one for the results of the War. The Germans would not have met with any special difficulties in making such a break through, as the German weak forces, without any assistance from the General Headquarters, took Kovno and broke through the Russian lines.

On the Russian side there was now a change in the Chief Command of the Army ; the Tzar gave in to the persuasions of his spouse, dismissed the Grand Duke Nicolai-Nicolaievich, and undertook the Chief Command himself.

The first measure is a question open to dispute ; it is quite true that the Grand Duke had caused incredible loss of human life, without attaining the slightest tactical successes. On the other hand he was a good soldier, who kept strict discipline. He was respected in the Army, and feared in the higher grades of the Service and especially at the front, for the strict measures he had introduced to maintain discipline. Perhaps he would have found ways and means to prevent the Bolshevik propaganda from penetrating into the Army.

The Tzar's second measure, the undertaking the Chief Command himself, can only be called a mistake. The work of a Commander-in-Chief in our

I

days requires the whole attention of a very capable man ; a monarch of a great country has not the time to devote to it, as the business of his government require both time and work from him daily. Either the leadership of the Army or the government of the country must suffer if he tries to do both.

CHAPTER X

FALKENHAYN AND SALONICA

ALREADY long before the fighting was drawing to an end in the Summer of 1915 the German General Headquarters had sent to the Danube any forces that could be spared from the German front to be brought into action against Serbia. Other units were despatched to the West and arrived there just in time to repulse the mighty attack made by the Entente.

The campaign against Serbia was necessary first, to relieve the pressure on Austria, secondly, in order to clear a direct way to Constantinople to send assistance to our Turkish Ally who was fighting desperately. The negotiations with Bulgaria had at last been settled. The Bulgarians who had been robbed of the fruits of their victory over the Turks in the second Balkan War by the Serbs, the Greeks and the Rumanians, were burning for revenge and hoped by joining the Central Powers not only to obtain it, but also to get Macedonia and the Dobrudja.

Before the commencement of the campaign there had again been a slight difference of opinion between the General Headquarters and General von Conrad. General von Conrad aimed at the entire destruction of the Serbian Army ; he proposed that the bulk of the Bulgarian troops should not be concentrated on the Timok, but farther South, so as to make it possible to cut off the entire Serbian Army that was being driven to the South by the armies of Mackensen and Kövesz. Unfortunately the German General Headquarters rejected this plan. In consequence of this the left wing of Mackensen's Army and the right wing of the Bulgarian Army very soon came into collision ; difficulties of marching and stoppages occurred, and part of the Serbian Army was able to escape.

It also seems incomprehensible that the campaign was not continued and Salonica captured as General von Conrad had recommended. That an advance on Salonica was technically impossible, which was the reason that General von Falkenhayn gave Conrad for not doing it, is not the truth. The opinion of the Chief of the Field Railways, Gröner, who was sent to Serbia specially to examine the matter proves quite clearly just the contrary ; it is equally useless to point to the neutrality of Greece as the cause ; the neutrality of Greece was violated when the Entente landed troops at Salonica. If we had driven the troops that had been landed there into the sea we should not have increased the difficulties of the position for Greece ; on the contrary, they would have been rendered less difficult.

I cannot share the opinion given by General Ludendorff (page 133 of his book) that if Salonica had been taken, the Serbians, Englishmen and Frenchmen who had been there would probably have fought on the West front, while we on our side would not have any Bulgarians there, and therefore to take or not to take Salonica was unimportant.

In the councils of the Entente there were different opinions as to whether the bridgehead of Salonica was still to be held after the attack from that point for the support of Serbia had failed, owing to the victory of the 2nd Bulgarian Army.

The capture of Salonica would probably have caused the Entente to give up their plans against Bulgaria, and it would have been possible to employ the Bulgarian troops elsewhere. They might have been brought into action against Rumania, and Rumania might have been forced either to join the Central Powers or at least to pursue a policy of benevolent neutrality.

Thus the Salonica front continued to exist, which forced us to keep troops in Macedonia, and at last, in 1918, caused the entire collapse of our Bulgarian Ally.

The limited objective that General von Falkenhayn had in view for the Serbian Campaign—to open out a way to Constantinople—was certainly attained, and even before the railway connexion with Constantinople had been opened, in the middle of January, as the Entente forces left Gallipoli on the 9th of January.

General von Falkenhayn only consented with reluctance to Conrad's plan of occupying Montenegro and Albania in order to clear the air in that direction and to prevent the Entente from making use of Montenegian territory as a military base for operations against Serbia. The execution of this plan met with no difficulties and on the 11th of January the Heights of Lovcen were stormed and Skutari was taken on the 30th of January.

In the meantime the Russians had attacked us again about Christmas. This time it was the extreme Southern wing that attacked the Southern Army, commanded by Linsinger, and the Austro-Hungarian 7th Army, under Pflanzer-Baltin. While the Southern Army repulsed every attack, the Army of Pflanzer-Baltin in the Bukowina fought with varying success, which continued until the middle of January. It was only with difficulty that their Army was able to maintain its position.

At the end of October the Commander-in-Chief in the East removed his Headquarters to Kovno.

During the advance the 12th and 8th Armies had been so closely pressed together that at last there was only space for one army, and the 12th remained. It was stationed on the Niemen as far North as the railway line Grodno-Mododeczno. As Commander-in-Chief General von Fabeck took over the command from General von Gallwitz, who had gone to Serbia. To the North of the 12th Army the 10th Army held the line as far as the Disna. Before Dvinsk a special Army Detachment was formed under the command of General von Scholtz, the former Commander-in-Chief of the 8th Army. From this point as far as the sea the Niemen Army, under General von Below, was stationed.

In order not to allow the name of the 8th Army, which was so closely connected with the fights in East Prussia, and especially with the battle of Tannenberg, to disappear, the Niemen Army was now named the 8th Army, and also, because the name of " Niemen Army " was, owing to its present position, no longer appropriate for it.

South of the position occupied by the Commander-in-Chief in the East the Army Group of Prince Leopold was stationed, which stretched out to the district South of Minsk. From this point Southwards the front was formed by the Austro-Hungarian Army Commands, with the Army Group of Linsingen on their left wing.

As soon as the fighting had ceased the work of constructing positions was carried on with the greatest energy. At the same time the reconstruction of the lines of connexion in the rear, especially the railways, was also undertaken. At the same time General Ludendorff created the admirable administrative organizations of the Commander-in-Chief in the East.

As the Russians, when they retired, had carried off with them the whole of the governing apparatus of the land, everything had to be created anew. These difficulties, however, had one advantage. There were no officials who could put obstacles in the way of the new administration.

The administrative district under the jurisdiction of the Commander-in-Chief in the East stretched much farther South than the military front extended, as it comprised the district occupied before by the 12th Army and now belonging to the provisional district of the Army Group of Prince Leopold of Bavaria, which included the forest of Bialovicz. The grandiose administration for the exploitation of timber that was established there by the Commissioner of Forests Escherich, who became so widely known after the War, can be cited as a good example of what was done.

I myself had nothing to do with the administration, and therefore, when the fighting gradually subsided, I had more free time which I employed in visiting the fronts and in becoming acquainted with them in detail. During these visits to the Army I saw all the most important sections of the front. Wherever I spoke with the troops in the trenches, I often was greatly stimulated by them ;

I learned the sorrows and cares of those men, and I was often able to help them.

Personal intercourse with the leaders of all grades also gave me valuable hints. Thus, when I visited the Niemen Army, the conversation turned for the first time on the possibility of capturing the Riga bridgehead. General von Below drew my attention to the crossing-place at Uxküll, and was the first to speak about operations at that point. Unfortunately we were unable to perform them in the Spring of 1916 and they were only executed in August, 1917.

CHAPTER XI

VERDUN INSTEAD OF ITALY

THE year 1915 had brought no decisive action on any of the fronts. We had maintained our positions in the West, and in the East we had had great successes. The decision that, in my opinion, might have been attained in the East had never been attempted by the German General Headquarters. The Austro-Hungarian Army Command had driven back all the attacks of the Italians ; by the Serbian defeat their rear had been freed from enemies, their self-confidence was increased in consequence of the events on the Russian front, especially as Pflanzer-Baltin's weak army had succeeded in keeping their positions without any German help. Now the question arose in both Allied Headquarters in what way was the campaign of 1916 to be continued.

Already in December, 1915, General von Conrad had requested the German General Headquarters to send him nine Divisions to Galicia in order to enable him to release a similar number of Austrian Divisions from that front, which he wanted to send to the Italian front to make a decisive attack on the Italians. General von Falkenhayn had refused to do so.

The German General Headquarters did not agree with the opinion that an attack on Italy and even a great defeat of the Italian Army would have any considerable effect on the general course of the War. On the other hand, they did not feel themselves strong enough to attempt decisive operations on any one of the fronts, as General von Falkenhayn has specifically stated in his book. It is quite possible to agree with him, as far as the negative portion of his explanation goes, that we were too weak, both in troops and material, to attempt a decisive attack or to break through any one of the enemy fronts.

In the East we had missed our chance, as has already often been asserted. As long as such considerable German forces were employed in the East it was impossible to bring together sufficient reserves in the West to make it possible to effect a break through on a large scale.

I cannot agree with General von Falkenhayn's conclusion from these facts, that it was therefore necessary to attack the strongest enemy—the French —at one point of the front. The French could not give up this position for reasons of prestige—they were therefore obliged to concentrate all the forces they could muster at that point. To attack the French without having the intention of attempting to bring about a decisive action, but only with the hope of weakening them, was a mistake. The unfortunate Verdun attempt had cost the French much loss of blood, but our losses were also very great indeed and in the end the French could justly reckon Verdun as a French victory. Operations that have only a limited object must only be undertaken when their success is certain. Verdun could only have been a success for the Germans had they been able to take the fortress.

The tragic side of this, as of so many other opportunities of this War, is that a success was nevertheless possible for us if the attack had been made in the proper way, that is, if the attack had been made simultaneously on both sides of the Meuse.   The attack on the Eastern bank alone was fated to come to a standstill as soon as it got under the flank fire from the other bank.   The French were really about to abandon at least the Eastern bank in consequence of our attack.   When, however, the 3rd Army Corps was brought to a standstill by the fire in their flank from the Western bank, they changed their plans.   What the reasons were that had prevented the attack on both banks, I do not know ; if it were want of troops, then the attack should not have been made at all.   My standpoint is different to General von Falkenhayn's : I would not have rejected General von Conrad's plan.   If it were impossible to deal a decisive blow on the chief front, I would have transferred the operations to Italy, the secondary theatre of War, but I would have made an attack there on a grand scale.   Judging by the success that the 11th German Army really had in 1917, if the attack General von Conrad had proposed making from Arsiero-Asiago had been executed simultaneously with a similar attack from Flitsch-Tolmein it might have led to a decisive defeat of the Italians.   Naturally it is impossible to say if such a defeat would have caused the Italians to seek for peace, still despite the pressure that England exercised on the Allies, the outbreak of internal troubles might have led to it.   If we had succeeded in continuing our offensive to the lines Genoa-Venice the results would have been very great not only for Italy, but through its effects on the Western front for France also.

Of course Austria-Hungary had the chief interest

in a great campaign against Italy—but we were so closely united—for better for worse with the Dual Monarchy that there was no use in swearing at the defective help rendered by the Allied troops ; on the contrary, we ought to have tried to raise the self-confidence and prestige of the Austro-Hungarian Army.

The first condition for a great attack on Italy was naturally the certainty that both the chief fronts in France and Russia would be held, as we had to be prepared in such a case, on both these fronts, for the Entente to make great attacks in order to relieve the pressure from Italy.   The most critical point would be the Austro-Hungarian sector of the Eastern front.   It would have been possible to extend the command of the Commander-in-Chief in the East as far as the Carpathians as it was afterwards done in the year 1916.   He would then have been in the position of sending to the most important places on the Austro-Hungarian front German reinforcements to strengthen the line and to place his scanty reserves behind the lines in such a way that they might intervene at the right moment.   Only once during the whole War were we taken by surprise on the Eastern front by a Russian attack—it was on the Aa in the winter of 1916-17— with this exception we were always warned by the wireless messages of the Russian staff of the positions where troops were being concentrated for any new undertaking.

Naturally this extension of the sphere where the Commander-in-Chief of the East had authority would not have pleased the Austro-Hungarian High Command.   The proposal would, at first, have met with opposition, as it was in 1916, when this plan was carried out, only owing to the pressure of circumstances. If, however, it had been explained to General von Conrad that it was only under these conditions that the offensive against Italy could be made with German assistance, and he had realized that he could strike such a destructive blow against Italy—the old hereditary enemy of Austria, only in this way, I certainly think he would have been willing seriously to consider the question of his submission to a higher authority.

However, as the circumstances really were at the time, Falkenhayn's jealousy of Hindenburg and Ludendorff would probably have placed more difficulties in the way of increasing the sphere of authority of both those generals than Conrad's scruples of allowing a great portion of the Eastern front to pass under German command would have done.

In fact, a consultation—which would have been most desirable—on the proposed operations never took place between the Chiefs of the General Staffs. It is true that General von Conrad had communicated his Italian projects, when he had asked for the assistance of German troops ; but General von Falkenhayn left the Allies in complete darkness about his own plans.

The German attacks on Verdun were at once answered by attacks of the Entente on all the fronts to relieve the pressure there. The Italians attacked Isonzo, for the fifth time in vain—and the Russians began an attack on a large scale on the front of the Commander-in-Chief in the East. Their attack was made in grand style, in the second half of March, and with such an expenditure of ammunition as we had not as yet seen in the East. It is, therefore, probable that this attack was not simply made to relieve the pressure at Verdun, but was part of the Entente's general plan of attack for 1916, that had been prepared with the object of breaking through our lines. But it had probably been begun sooner than they had intended, with the object of relieving the Western front. It is otherwise not possible to suppose that without this compulsion they would have begun so early as March, when the notorious " roadlessness " obtains in those parts. In Russia the period which often lasts for weeks, when the colossal quantities of snow begin to melt, is called " roadless," as communications, except on the highways, which in Russia are few and far between, are rendered impossible.

The point of attack was well chosen. The chief assault was made between the lakes Viszniev and Narocz on the one side and Postavz on the other. This double attack was to envelop the German 21st Corps from both sides, run them down and thus make a wide breach through the line towards Vilna and Kovno. Secondary attacks—probably chiefly to detain the German reserves and to divert the attention of the German Command—were made to the South of Dvinsk, near Vidzy, at Dvinsk and at Yakobstadt. The attack began on the 15th of March with a drum-fire, such as we had never experienced in the East before.

From the 18th to the 21st, and later again on the 26th, there were infantry attacks that were conducted, as usual, bravely and obstinately and with utter disregard for the loss of life.

Unfortunately, a Baden reserve regiment was overpowered between the two lakes. This produced a temporary crisis at that place. However somewhat further to the rear the 10th Army succeeded in warding off the blow and in closing the line again. All the other attacks were repulsed with great losses for the Russians.

Our thin lines fought as usual admirably. Naturally there were some exciting moments at Postavy, but there is never a battle without such moments.   Towards the end of March the attacks subsided.   With the exception of a small area near Lake Narocz the German positions had all been retained.

By the beginning of April quiet set in along the whole Eastern front.   At the end of April we re-captured our lost positions on Lake Narocz.   This attack of the 10th Army which was preceded by an admirably carried out artillery preparation, can serve as an example of all our subsequent attacks in the East.   The artillery preparation was in the charge of the Commander of the artillery of a Land-wehr Division, the retired Lieutenant-Colonel Bruch-müller.   This artillery officer, who afterwards be-came famous, not only in the East, but in the whole Army, was discovered then.

I consider Bruchmüller to be quite a genius in his way.   He had a gift, which I have never seen possessed by any other artillery officer, of knowing, as if by instinct, the exact quantity of ammunition that it was necessary to discharge on any single point to render it ready to be stormed.   The troops also soon noticed that an attack which had previously been prepared by artillery under Bruchmüller's command was a sure thing, and they advanced with full confidence in the success of any undertaking that had been prepared by the artillery of Bruch-müller and his staff.

From all the reports that came in it appeared

that notwithstanding the attacks that had been repulsed at Postavz-Narocz, the Russian Headquarters was planning an attack on the front of the Commander-in-Chief in the East. Large concentration of troops and preparations for an attack, the reports said, were being made at Smorgon, at Dvinsk and at the Riga bridgehead.

The General Headquarters had placed several Divisions from the South front at the disposal of the Commander-in-Chief in the East. These Divisions as well as our own reserves, were stationed at the points necessary for meeting the expected attack, and we awaited with full confidence the Russian preparations for an offensive.

The Commander-in-Chief in the East would have been better pleased if he had been able to forestall the Russian attack by an advance from our side. The most desirable point of attack for us would have been Riga. It was impossible to do so with our own forces, even with the above mentioned reserves that the General Headquarters had sent us : we would not have been strong enough. The numerical superiority of the Russians was enormous. The bridgehead of Riga was the most sensitive point in the front of the Commander-in-Chief in the East. If the Russians had succeeded in making an attack from that bridgehead somewhere in the direction of Mitau the whole of the front of the Commander-in-Chief in the East would have had to retire.

As a preventive measure against such an attack the Headquarters of the Commander-in-Chief in the East began, therefore, to consider the plan, originally suggested by General Otto von Below, of crossing the Dvina at Uxküll. Had the General

Headquarters been in a position to give us some six Divisions more, it might have been possible to carry this plan into effect. It offered not only the possibility of capturing the Riga bridgehead, but likewise of dealing a severe blow to the whole Russian Army. If we succeeded by a surprise attack in crossing the Dvina at Uxküll and then of making a thrust Northwards as far as the sea, the chief part of the Russian garrison at the Riga bridgehead would be cut off. The fall of Riga would be a moral victory, and the German positions from Uxküll to the sea would be considerably shorter than they were, so that the necessity for more troops was only temporary ; they would soon be free, and besides the Commander-in-Chief in the East would be able to spare some of the forces he had owing to the much shorter line of his front.

On the other hand, the Russians would be obliged to concentrate more reserves at that point and it would probably have prevented them from resuming the offensive, at least for a time, on the Eastern front.

The fall of Riga could not have produced a battle that would have decided the fate of the campaign, but it would have been a fine success that would have raised the spirits of the Army and could have been obtained with probably but little loss, and would have contributed to the gradual defeat of the Russian Army.

About the end of May H.M. the Kaiser, accompanied by the Chief of the General Staff, came to Kovno in order to go over the territories under the administration of the Commander-in-Chief in the East. The Commander-in-Chief explained the Riga plan and requested the assignment of the six

K

Divisions that were needed. Unfortunately, His Majesty was obliged to refuse the request. General von Falkenhayn explained that he required all the troops at Verdun. Verdun was a great success, and it was to be presumed that during the continuation of the fights, the bulk of the French Army would be ground down in the mill of Verdun.

General Ludendorff and I were not of that opinion ; but our opinion was not sufficient to alter the decision already taken.

Whether the General Headquarters was able to give the six Divisions is difficult to decide, but I think it would have been possible, as a few weeks later, at the collapse of the Austrian front, it was obliged to send, and sent, about the same number of Divisions to support it.

In May the grinding battle of Verdun was continued in the West. With this exception both on the Western and Eastern fronts there was quiet ; only in Mesopotamia fighting was going on after the Turks had succeeded at the end of April in taking Kut-el-Amara.

On the 15th of May, General von Conrad began his offensive in Italy. For weeks he had had to wait on account of the weather. With a powerful rush the Army of the Arch-Duke Eugene broke out of the line Rovereto-Trieste, swept the Italians from the mountains and burst through the enemy's line of frontier forts between Arsiero-Arsigo.

By the end of May the Army was fighting for the last mountain ridges that still barred the way to the plains and which were obstinately defended by the Italians.

It was only a question of days or even of hours before the struggle for this passage would have been consummated.

In the Staff of the Commander-in-Chief in the East we were discussing with the Austro-Hungarian liaison officer the future prospects, when on the 4th of June the great battle that took place in the Southern half of the Eastern front against the Austro-Hungarians, completely changed the fairly favourable picture of the year 1916.

As it became known by Colonel Blood's article in the *Quarterly Review*, of October, 1920, the Entente had intended to make a general attack on the German Army during the Summer of 1916, which was to begin on the 1st of July in the West on the Somme, in the East at Baranoviczi-Smorgon.

The chief attacks against Baranoviczi-Smorgon were to be supported by auxiliary attacks at Riga and also at Luck, Tarnopol, and on the Dniester. It has already been stated that these Russian concentrations of troops and preparations for an attack on the front of the Commander-in-Chief in the East had been noticed and correctly understood.

The Austro-Hungarian attack in Italy caused the Russians, in response to a request made by the Italians, to begin the intended auxiliary attack on the Austro-Hungarian front before they had intended, and it unexpectedly brought the Russians the most brilliant victory they had in the whole campaign.

When, on the 4th of June, the Russians, who were numerically scarcely superior to the Austro-Hungarian troops, and who had neither concentrated their forces at any special point for the attack, nor made any great artillery preparation for it, fell upon the 4th Army at Lutsk and the 7th in the Bukovina, both these Armies gave way helplessly without offering any serious resistance.   The retreat of the 4th Army, more especially, soon assumed the character of a rout. Unfortunately the leadership of General von Linsingen and his Chief of the General Staff Stoltzmann was not equal to the situation ; it entirely failed, and was mainly the cause of the greatness of this disaster.

On the 7th of June the Russians took Lutsk, on the 13th their vanguard reached Stochod, Southeast of Kovel. During the first three days more than 200,000 Austrians were made prisoners.

This unexpected success caused the Russian Headquarters to change their plans. They gave up the attack that had been planned on the front of the Commander-in-Chief in the East, which after the experiences they had had in March at Postavy they were probably not looking forward to with much confidence, and they gradually took troops away from our front and sent them to the South to increase the success they had already achieved there. This decision can appear comprehensible, but it was not right. If, on the contrary, the Russians had now attacked the German front with all their forces, regardless of the losses they might incur, they would have prevented the Commander-in-Chief in the East from sending forces for the support of our Allies, and without this help the crisis would probably have developed into a complete defeat of the Austro-Hungarian Army.

The measures taken by the Commander-in-Chief in the East would have had greater effect if the conditions of the Command on the Eastern front had been more homogeneous. And although the personal relations with the Army Group of Prince Leopold of Bavaria and with the Army Detachment Woyrsch, which was chiefly affected by the Russian attack, were excellent, especially with Colonel Heye, the Chief of the Staff of the Army Detachment Woyrsch, with whom a constant exchange of ideas took place, still all sorts of friction occurred, owing to the wish of the General Headquarters that all intercourse between the various sections of the Army should be effected through them and not directly.

On the receipt of the first reports of the collapse of the Austro-Hungarian 4th Army, the Commander-in-Chief in the East had several Divisions prepared to be transported to the South, although at that time he had to reckon with the possibility of strong Russian attacks. The Army Group of Prince Leopold of Bavaria made similar preparations.

The troops that were sent were naturally not sufficient. The General Headquarters found themselves obliged to send strong forces from the Western front for the support of the Allied Army. Once again we have the picture we have seen so often before : if the General Headquarters had given the Commander-in-Chief in the East the six Divisions he asked for in order to capture the Riga bridgehead at the proper time, it is probable that the whole of the Russian attack would not have taken place, and the Summer of 1916 would have ended with a great German success on the Eastern front ; now they were obliged to give the six Divisions in order to avert a great disaster that menaced the whole of that front.

To take strong forces away from the West, when to judge by all the information that came in, the Entente's great attack on the Somme was imminent, was a difficult decision to make, but it was not to be avoided. General von Conrad had instantly stopped the whole of the Italian offensive and he had dispatched troops from the Italian front to the East. The first thing that had to be done was to stop the attack near Lutsk. As soon as the first reinforcements arrived the General Headquarters tried to stop the Austro-Hungarian troops by making a counter attack, but the resisting powers of the Austro-Hungarian 4th Army was too much shaken. The first German troops were carried off in the retreat.

The next German reinforcements that arrived first formed a new front on the Stockod and stopped the Russian pursuit. The next troops that came took up the remains of the 4th Army near Kisjelin and South of that place in the district round Gorochov. They formed with them a strong group for attack, and commenced an advance from that place. As on the one hand the reinforcements only arrived in driblets, owing to the defective state of the railway communications, and on the other the critical position did not admit of a delay the offensive was begun with insufficient forces and they had no decisive success. At all events the Russian advance was stopped here. It was an advantage for us that the Russian attack had been made without proper preparation, and had no strong reserves in its rear, and therefore was quickly brought to a standstill by the resistance that was opposed to it.

The position of the 7th Army in the Bukovina resembled that of the 4th Army, though it was not quite so bad. The front was broken through in several places, the Russians took Czernowitz and had reached the line Dniester-Kolomea-Kimpolung by the end of June. The line of the Austro-Hungarian front that before the Russian attack had occupied the narrow strip of land between the Rumanian frontier to the East of Czernowitz and the Dniester was, owing to the retreat, greatly increased in length. Owing to the bad means of communication it was difficult to send them reinforcements and they were long in arriving, although both from the German and the Austro-Hungarian sides everything was done that was possible to hasten their arrival. It was lucky for us that the Russians suffered from the same difficulties of transport, and here also the want of preparation for the attack and the absence of reserves prevented them from following up their success with energy.

On the 13th of June the Russians began a strong attack on the Army Detachment Woyrsch at Baranovici. This was followed by a series of exciting days. But with the exception of a small breach made in the line of one of the Austro-Hungarian Divisions, the Army Detachment was able successfully to repulse all the attacks. However, they had to employ their last reserves for this purpose, and the Commander-in-Chief in the East had likewise to send the last of the troops he had at his disposal to assist them. By doing this the Commander-in-Chief in the East ran a certain risk, as the Russians who were facing his front, notwithstanding that they had begun dispatching troops to the South, were still quite strong enough to attack him. In fact the Russians did attack the front of the Commander-in-Chief in the East at Lake Narocz, Smorgon, Dvinsk Friedrichstadt and at the Riga bridgehead. Most of these attacks were little more than demonstrations and they were easily repulsed. Their object was only to mask the dispatch of Russian forces to the South, and to prevent us from sending reinforcements there too. Only at Riga was the attack fiercer ; by making a strong thrust the Russians were at first able to capture some territory. However the bravery of the troops and the good leadership of the 8th Army soon regained the lost positions.

The reserves that had been sent to the South from the front of the Commander-in-Chief of the East gave renewed energy to the attack on the Brussilov front. The ground that had been gained by German counter attacks in the Lutsk angle had partially to be given up. General von Böhm-Ermolly, the Commander of the Austro-Hungarian 2nd Army, was obliged to retire with his left wing and centre to the Galician frontier.

The Russian attacks on the Styr, to the North of Lutsk, were also successful. The Austro-Hungarian troops gave way here. General von Linsingen found himself obliged to draw back his left wing beyond the Stochod. The right wing of the Army Group of Prince Leopold of Bavaria had likewise to retire to the South of the Pripet.

The position had become very critical for the whole of the Eastern front. The uncertainty concerning our Allies was what mostly told on our nerves. Nowhere was it certain, if the Russians attacked, that they would be able to hold out. We scraped together all the reserves we could find, thinned the quieter fronts and obtained in this way a few regiments. By these means we were able to send some reinforcements to Linsingen's Army Group, which enabled him to hold the Stochod. This was successful, and the chief crisis was thus tided over.

Count Bothmer, the Commander of the German

Southern Army—the Chief of whose General Staff was Colonel von Hemmer, a very able man—also found himself obliged, at the beginning of June, owing to the complete failure of our Allies, to draw his right wing back to the South of the Dniester, but in his new positions he repulsed every Russian attack as he had done before in his old ones.

The events that had occurred thus far proved the unsuitability of the existing division of the Chief Command, as well as the necessity of mixing the Allies more closely on the front. Wherever German troops were stationed, or where the Austro-Hungarian troops were intermixed with German ones, every Russian attack was repulsed and our front had been held. Wherever the Allied troops had alone held a long front they had failed.

The Commander-in-Chief in the East had already pointed this out. At the end of June Field-Marshal von Hindenburg and General Ludendorff were summoned to the General Headquarters in the West. They again pointed out the necessity of a strict unity of the chief command on the whole of the Eastern front as it was only possible by those means to manage with the limited number of reserves we possessed. They also proposed to send more German troops to the Austrian front. In order to do this weak Austrian Divisions could be posted at quiet places on the front of the Commander-in-Chief in the East and by so doing German Divisions could be freed to be employed on the Austro-Hungarian front.

The first proposal of having a single Commander-in-Chief on the Eastern front as far as the Carpathians they were unable to carry through. As General von Falkenhayn mentions in his book he never even suggested the question to the Allies; he tried to obtain a German Chief Command on the Southern half of the Eastern front under General von Mackensen. By dividing the Chief Command between two on the Eastern front naturally not much would have been attained.

The sending of Austro-Hungarian Divisions to the front of the Commander-in-Chief in the East was effected in a limited measure. The first that arrived was a war-worn Infantry Division which was stationed in the neighbourhood of Lake Narocz, and for which General von Linsingen was given in exchange the 10th Landwehr Division.

At the end of July Field-Marshal von Hindenburg and General Ludendorff were again ordered to go to the General Headquarters. The difficult position on the Eastern front demanded energetic measures. The fall of Brody, news of which had just arrived, caused most of the little objections to be silenced. They were unable as yet to decide on complete measures and to extend the front of the Commander-in-Chief in the East as far as the Carpathians; they decided, however, to place under his command the whole front as far as the district South of Brody, that is to include the Army Group of Böhm-Ermolly.

The Army of Pflanzer-Baltin, the Austro-Hungarian 3rd Army and the Southern Army were formed into a new Army Group under the command of the Arch-Duke Heir Apparent Karl. He was given as Chief of the General Staff the German General von Seeckt.

Although these new arrangements of the Chief Command were only half measures, still they denoted an improvement.

The Commander-in-Chief in the East began his

new duties by first visiting the new positions that were now under his command in order to acquaint himself with the state of affairs on the spot. The Chief Command of the 10th and 8th Army Groups was undertaken by General von Eichhorn retaining the command of the 10th and his Headquarters at Vilna.

The 12th Army was joined to the Army Group of Prince Leopold of Bavaria.

Before he had had time to have personal conversations with the leaders of the Southern portion of the Eastern front, the Russians recommenced the attack along the whole front.

On the 25th and 27th of July, the Russians, in great numbers, made a fierce attack on Baranovice, but they were repulsed.

For Linsingen's Army Group fighting had never ceased on the Stochod. From the 28th of July to the 1st of August fierce attacks were made on this front which, quite regardless of the losses they sustained, the Russians were determined to break through at all costs. It came to a crisis at many points, but on the whole the line held out. The attacks had also spread to the Southern part of Gronau's Army Detachment which joined on to the left wing of Linsingen's Army Group ; but they were all repulsed at once. It was thought probable that the attacks would be extended farther South and that they would spread to the Army Group of Böhm-Ermolly and to the troops under the command of Arch-Duke Karl.

The Staffs we visited were consequently in very low spirits.

General Ludendorff, who had to arrange for the removal of the Staff from Kovno to a place more suitable for the Headquarters of the newly extended sphere of the Commander-in-Chief in the East, had only taken the smaller and exclusively military staff with him and had gone with them temporarily to Brest-Litovsk. Geographically Brest-Litovsk was the most suitable place for the new Headquarters, but the town had been entirely burnt down and could not provide quarters for the whole Staff of the Commander-in-Chief in the East. The only part of the town that was still in existence was the officers' quarters in the Citadel; they were dirty and neglected, too, but offered the possibility of being rendered inhabitable in a short time. The space that could be disposed of was just sufficient for the military portion of the Staff, but the administrative section of the Staff of the Commander-in-Chief in the East had to remain in Kovno. Until the necessary cleaning up and arrangements could be made we lived in our train at the Brest-Litovsk Station.

On the 3rd and 4th of August, General Field-Marshal von Hindenburg, General Ludendorff and I went to Kowel to see General von Linsingen, and the next day to Vladimir-Volynsk to the Commander-in-Chief of the Austro-Hungarian Army, Colonel-General von Tertczanski, and then to Lemberg, to the 2nd Austro-Hungarian Army to see General von Böhm-Ermolly and his Chief of Staff, General Bardolf.

On the way back to Brest-Litovsk we also spoke to the Generals von der Maritz and Lietzmann, the Commanders of the Groups of Austro-Hungarian and German troops that formed part of the Linsingen Group. The German Generals spoke of the position as very serious. The fronts were thin, strong Russian attacks could be expected, most of the Austro-Hungarian units could not be relied on, but everywhere we found firm determination and confidence to be able to hold out.

The reports of the Austro-Hungarian leaders were also not calculated to throw a more rosy light on the picture. General von Tertczanski admitted quite openly that his troops had not the necessary inner moral firmness, and that they were scarcely in a position to resist a strong Russian attack.

The same unsatisfactory picture was given by General von Seeckt of the condition of the Army Group of the Arch-Duke Heir Apparent Karl. General Ludendorff had summoned General von Seeckt to Lemberg for a consultation.

Böhm-Ermolly and Burdorf were slightly more confident. Only on one point all four were of one mind : in the demand for German troops in order to intermix them with the Austro-Hungarian units.

The Commander-in-Chief in the East was unable to assist much in that way at first. The strong Russian attacks at Riga had been repulsed for the time, but it was not impossible that they would be renewed.

As has already been remarked, Riga was the most sensitive spot of the whole of the Northern front ; if the Russians could succeed in breaking through there, the whole of the front would have to retire. We were unable to take away the 1st Landwehr Division that we still had at our disposal there. With great trouble we had been able to draw from the rest of the front three battalions more, one Artillery Detachment under Major-General Melior, to form a reserve and also one reinforced Cavalry Brigade.

During the consultations at Lemberg General Ludendorff had promised to send Melior's Detachment to the 2nd Austro-Hungarian Army so that for the whole front from Lemberg to Riga all the reserves that the Commander-in-Chief in the East had at his disposal was one Cavalry Brigade. This Brigade was afterwards also sent to the 2nd Austro-Hungarian Army.

The General Headquarters had three Divisions still at their disposal. These had been newly formed during July from parts of units that the Western front had sent to other fronts, and they were destined for the Eastern front. They had likewise the disposal of a Turkish Army Corps that Enver Pasha had promised. The arrival of this Corps could, however, not be counted on, as only one train a day had been assigned for its transport. It was afterwards placed at the disposal of the South Army under Count Bothmer and in conjunction with it had fought splendidly.

We would gladly have disposed of the German Divisions of the General Headquarters. General Ludendorff begged that they might be sent quickly. Unfortunately the General Headquarters delayed for several days before they were dispatched. In consequence of this the Commander-in-Chief in the East was prevented from averting a misfortune that befell the Army Group Böhm-Ermolly.

In the meantime the Russian Headquarters had come to the conclusion that it was hopeless to try to break through the German front, and their next attacks were made South of the Pripet. During the days from the 8th to the 10th of August the Army Group Linsingen and the left wing of the Army Detachment Gronau were again subjected to fierce attacks. Most of these attacks were repulsed, with the exception of two places, at Toboly and Kisielin, on the Western bank of the Stochod, which the Russians succeeded in taking and retaining.

Simultaneously with these attacks the Russians attacked the 2nd Austro-Hungarian Army and Arch-Duke Karl's Army Group. The right wing of the Austro-Hungarian Army was broken through and had to give up its positions on the Sereth. It was only now that the General Headquarters placed two of the three Divisions—the 195th and 197th—at the disposal of the Commander-in-Chief in the East which were brought into action under the command of General von Eben. They succeeded in stopping the retreat of the Austro-Hungarian troops at Zborow and after hard fighting and severe losses they were permanently brought to a stand.

Melior's Detachment had already previously been brought into action.

Unfortunately the Russians also had succeeded against Arch-Duke Karl's troops. They broke through his lines at Tlumacz and took Nadworna and Stanislau. As the Austro-Hungarian troops had given way on both his wings Count Bothmer was obliged to withdraw the Southern Army, which had repulsed every attack of the Russians, beyond the Zlota-Lipa. The Russian attacks on the Carpathian passes were all driven back owing to the assistance of German troops. Nevertheless the impression produced by this great defeat of the Austro-Hungarian Army near the Rumanian frontier was so great that it removed the last hesitation Rumania still had of joining the enemy Confederation. Her attitude became with every day more suspicious, and it became necessary to count upon her entering the War on the side of our enemies.

After the round the Commander-in-Chief in the East had made to visit the Staffs that had been newly placed under his command, we passed several days in our train at the Brest-Litovsk Station and then, about the middle of August, removed to the Citadel. When I unpacked my trunk I little thought that my stay there would last nearly two years. There was an enormous amount of work that devolved upon every department of the Staff. Not only had General Ludendorff undertaken to keep tactical order in the East, but also to raise the conditions of the training in the Austro-Hungarian Army, and he went into the matter with his usual energy.

On the 29th of August I had to be at a conference in East Prussia. Shortly before I left Brest there was a telephone call from the Chief of the Military Cabinet, Baron Lincker, which summoned Field-Marshal von Hindenburg and General Ludendorff to the General Headquarters. Owing to their departure I had some hesitation about absenting myself at the same time, but as I was only to be away one night, I decided to go and it was in Insterburg that on the 29th of August I received the news that General Field-Marshal von Hindenburg had been appointed Chief of the General Staff of the field forces and General Ludendorff to be first Quartermaster-General. The new Commander-in-Chief in the East was General Field-Marshal Prince Leopold of Bavaria, and I was appointed his Chief of the General Staff.

Thus ended a period of two years during which I had worked together with General Ludendorff, an epoch rich in work, rich in cares, but also rich in successes. During the whole of that time no discordant note had ever troubled the work we had to do together, and I believe and hope that the friendship which was established between us by the experiences of those hard years can never be shaken. It has often been asserted that I had taken it amiss that General Ludendorff had not taken me with him to the General Headquarters. I wish to deny most emphatically all these rumours. I leave it an open question whether our union, which during two years had been without the slightest friction, would have been for the general good if it had been continued longer. For me the nomination as Chief of the General Staff of the Commander-in-Chief in the East was naturally a great distinction and a better post. It gave me a position of responsibility.

The distinction of being Chief of the General Staff was nearly cut short. The extra train that was taking me on the 29th from East Prussia back to Brest-Litovsk, by a mistake of the engine-driver, ran into a furlough train to the North of Bialystock. There were quite a number of injured. I myself escaped with only a painful shaking.

L

CHAPTER XII

THE POLISH ARMY THAT FAILED TO APPEAR, AND THE SUBMARINE WAR WITHOUT SUBMARINES

BEFORE I begin a new chapter of my Reminiscences as Chief of the General Staff, I wish to say a few words on two questions, although I neither had any influence on their development nor on their settlement. These questions, however, were often discussed by the Staff of the Commander-in-Chief, especially when statesmen, or persons who thought they were statesmen and politicians from the centre of the Empire came to visit us : they are the Polish question and the question of the Submarine War.

I do not know who first suggested the idea of creating a Polish Kingdom ; I think it was Baron Burian, who eventually signed the agreement with the Chancellor of the Empire, Bethmann-Hollweg. It was a stupid idea—it deprived the Tzar of any possibility of concluding a separate peace—and it was quite superfluous. There was not the slightest reason for the Central Powers to touch on the Polish question. The creation of a General Government of Warsaw by Germany and a General Government of Lublin by Austria-Hungary were already mistakes as they seemed to give to these Polish provinces which had been taken from Russia a special status.

It would have been better to have treated these provinces in the same way as the other portions of the Russian Empire occupied by the Allied Armies, and to have simply made them the zones of occupation of the army in question.

General Ludendorff had often talked with me about the idea of founding a new Polish Kingdom, and he always declared that in answer to questions regarding this matter he had said he could only agree to the plan if the Poles could assist the Central Powers with an Army that, at first, must be at least four Divisions strong. I was sceptical about Polish auxiliary troops, but at that time we were so much in want of reserves, that from a military point of view, we looked with pleasure on any accessions we could obtain.

The advisability of the formation of a Polish Army was encouraged by those who were of the opinion that it was a pitiable idea that so numerous a nation as the Poles should suffer their freedom and independence should be obtained only by the struggles of others, without themselves making any sacrifices in the cause. It is well known now that we soldiers deceived ourselves, and the politicians did not make the military demands one of the conditions of the political bargain.

With regard to the question of the U-boats, no man of sense can be in doubt that in our struggle for the existence of Germany, we not only had every right, but that it was our bounden duty to bring them into action without any consideration for others. It is absurd to talk of inhumanity and that sort of thing, when all know that England had already begun the hunger blockade against German women and children. There was no possibility for us Germans to escape from the consequences of this blockade, while the Americans had no need to take their pleasure trips exactly in zones blockaded by Germany. From the very beginning I was only afraid that we might commence the U-boat war too soon, that is to say, we would not have sufficient submarines to be able to continue this warfare. I often think of a discussion I had on this question with the President of the Union of Landowners, Dr. Rösicke, in Kovno, when he came to visit the Field-Marshal. During this discussion he reproached me with want of patriotism, etc., when I objected to bringing the unrestricted submarine warfare into immediate action.

Later events proved that I was right. We began too soon, that is, with too few U-boats, and the results were very similar to those produced by our Gas Warfare. We showed the adversary what a dangerous weapon we possessed at a time when the weapon was not strong enough to prevent him from taking the necessary measures to defend himself from it. I do not doubt that it would have been possible for the U-boat Warfare to have had a complete success if from the beginning of the War we had applied all our available power to the construction of innumerable submarines.

If, as Admiral Tirpitz says in his book, the Commanders of the Naval Warfare had determined from the beginning not to employ the fleet for a great decisive naval battle, it was quite useless to continue the construction of battleships during the War.

CHAPTER XIII

THE CONDITIONS OF MY NEW COMMAND

On the 30th of August I took over the business of the Chief of the General Staff of the Commander-in-Chief in the East. As my successor to the post of senior officer of the General Staff I had suggested to the General Headquarters the choice of two officers on the General Staff of the Eastern front, who according to their seniority I considered were the most suitable for this appointment. They were Lieutenant-Colonel Keller and Major Brinckmann ; both these men had special military capacities and extensive knowledge, extraordinary powers of work and fresh optimism.

At first Lieutenant-Colonel Keller was appointed, but he only remained a short time and then became the Chief of Linsingen's General Staff. His post was then occupied by Major Brinckmann who afterwards became very widely known owing to his participation in the Peace Negotiations of Brest-Litovsk and of the Armistice Negotiations in the West.

The new Commander-in-Chief arrived next day. Already before the War I had become acquainted with H.R.H. Field-Marshal Prince Leopold of Bavaria during the great manœuvres, when I had met him several times, and having heard his criticisms I knew that he was a clever soldier and a distinguished superior officer. During the two-and-a-half years that we worked together I found that these two qualities were his most conspicuous characteristics. The Prince was an impassioned soldier, a keen sportsman and rider and the last *Grandseigneur* I ever met. In the most difficult situations he retained a clear mind and iron nerves. During that whole time we never had any differences over military questions and I can only remember one case when the Prince did not reply to me with the amiability he usually showed to everybody. During the battle at Zloczov-Tarnopol, in July, 1917, H.R.H. had forced his way to the front, and he would have been best pleased if he could have been in the front line of infantry. We had taken up our positions with the 1st Guard Division on a small mound from which a general view of the battle could be obtained. The Russians began to direct their artillery on this mound. I felt it was my duty to beg the Prince to change his position as there was not the slightest use in our remaining there any longer, and it was to be expected that in a few minutes a strong artillery fire would pour on the spot where we were standing. Danger afforded the Prince pleasure. In answer to my energetic insistence he replied, in an almost unfriendly tone :

" You begrudge me the smallest pleasure."

From the other members of the Staff, General Ludendorff only took Major von Bockelberg with him to his new sphere of work. He had been Assistant Quartermaster-General and his place was now taken on the Staff of the Commander-in-Chief in the East by Major Hofmann, an officer of great military capacities, of incredible industry, love of work and an iron sense of duty.

The Administrative Departments remained as

formerly under the Chief Quartermaster-General, von Eisenhardt-Rothe. There was a small superficial difficulty here, as Eisenhardt-Rothe was already a General, while I, his chief, had only just been promoted to the rank of Colonel. This difficulty was quickly overcome, as General von Eisenhardt consented to work under me. We worked together without the slightest friction until, on my recommendation, General von Eisenhardt was appointed Quartermaster-General to the Commander-in-Chief. General von Eisenhardt added to profound knowledge and great culture in every branch, a special capacity for all administrative questions. In character, in a just feeling of responsibility and in demeanour, he was a perfect example of an old-fashioned Prussian officer, in the best meaning of the words.

H.R.H. took up his private quarters in the small abandoned estate Skoki. Every morning at about eleven o'clock he came to the office to hear the report, he had his mid-day meal at home, and in the evening at half-past seven he came to the mess dinner in the officers' quarters. However, he informed me, that from five a.m.—his usual hour of rising both in Summer and Winter—he was always at my disposal at any time if it were required.

The position on the front of the Commander-in-Chief in the East could be looked upon as in general safe at that time, though, of course, we had to expect new Russian attacks at any moment. The 195th and 197th Divisions under General von Eben, which had been sent to reinforce the Austro-Hungarian 2nd Army, had effectually succeeded in bringing it to a standstill. The last Russian attacks on

Woyrsch had also been successfully repulsed. There was still a certain tension in the Linsingen Army Group on the Stochod, though Colonel Hell, Linsingen's Chief of Staff, was quite confident for the future. The position was not quite so secure with the Arch-Duke Karl's Army Group, and there were hardly any forces at our disposal to repulse our new enemy—Rumania.

On the West fierce battles were raging on the Somme and at Verdun and were producing great gaps in the effectives of the German Army that could never be made good. For the first time the feeling of the absolute superiority of the German soldier was lost, and signs of war weariness and despondency began to be observable in certain quarters. The general situation was much more serious when Field-Marshal von Hindenburg and General Ludendorff undertook the Chief Command of the Army than it had been at the first change of that post after the battle of the Marne.

During the two years he had been Commander-in-Chief General von Falkenhayn had squandered the Capital he had had in the proud Army and the national enthusiasm, without having attained a single success. Ludendorff's energy was able to master these difficulties. The unfortunate Verdun adventure was liquidated ; the line of the Somme was held though with loss of territory ; the Arch-Duke Karl's Army was supported, and the troops that were necessary for the Rumanian campaign were created. The chief labour for the last task fell to the lot of the Commander-in-Chief in the East. Although, as already mentioned, the situation of the Linsingen Group was not quite secure, we gave as many troops as could be spared, and even more.

We drew off some regiments from quiet parts of the front and created new Divisions. The risks that were run by doing this had to be borne, and H.R.H. the Commander-in-Chief and I were quite willing to bear them.

Once again it was proved that the Russian Army had produced no great leader, no man of real strategic understanding. Instead of attacking us again along the whole front and occupying us in that way, to hinder us from removing troops to send to other fronts, Brussilov's offensive was absolutely stopped. The Russians dispatched their reserves to the South to take part in the Rumanian offensive.

At the time that the Chief Command of the Allied Armies was undertaken by the German Headquarters, new rules for the condition of the different Commands were made and the sphere of the Commander-in-Chief in the East was also slightly increased. The Southern Army of Count Bothmer was placed under his command. This Army and the Austro-Hungarian 2nd Army formed the Army Group of Böhm-Ermolly. Unfortunately the 3rd Austro-Hungarian Army, which was stationed to the immediate North of the Carpathians, was not as yet included in this arrangement.

However, even without this section, the front was large enough to occupy the whole of a man's working power. Even when there was no fighting my days passed in the following manner : In the morning I went to the office at eight o'clock, where I found the morning reports which usually necessitated instructions to be given ; about eleven o'clock H.R.H. the Commander-in-Chief came in to hear the report which took up a shorter or longer time according to circumstances. At one o'clock I went straight from the office to the mess-room to lunch; from two to three I took a walk of an hour, and then returned to the office where I remained until it was time to go to the mess dinner at half-past seven. H.R.H. remained after dinner for about half an hour in conversation with the members of the Staff and the guests who always were present. At nine o'clock he drove back to Skoki while I and the other members of the Staff returned to the office where we usually were occupied until one o'clock. If important engagements were in progress the working day was longer and the time of rest from one to seven was often disturbed by telegraphic or telephonic messages. Unfortunately my present occupations did not give me time to visit all the sections of the front as I had been able to do while I was chief assistant, and become acquainted with them by personal inspection. My work did not admit of such long absences. I therefore requested the Central Department of the General Staff to provide me with a very capable General Staff Officer whom I could entrust with the task of obtaining direct touch with the troops, and of getting closely acquainted with all the most important positions. I was very fortunate in this matter: the Central Department sent me an officer who had really remarkable capacities for the execution of this difficult task. Major Wachenfeld possessed both great tactical understanding and military penetration, united with the amiability and tactful reticence that are absolutely necessary for the fulfilment of his difficult task. He was untiring in making his inspections; he gave valuable encouragement to the troops at their posts, and he placed the Commander-in-Chief in the position of giving orders if it were necessary for taking steps to rectify any omissions that might have been made in the construction of the positions.

In the beginning of September Field-Marshal Hindenburg and General Ludendorff went for a short time from Pless to the Western theatre of War in order to be able to consult on the spot about the new position of affairs, especially on the Somme and at Verdun.   Shortly after this visit I came for one day to Pless for a consultation on questions regarding the Service.   The relations between General Ludendorff and myself were still, at that time, of the most friendly and confidential nature. He spoke quite openly of the serious position in the West, and that much had been neglected in the construction of the positions, and many mistakes had been made.   He said the General Headquarters and the War Office had not exerted sufficient pressure on the working capacity of our industries, for the production of the necessary war material, especially of ammunition, and that, in general, there had been a complete failure of a united effort of the General Headquarters and the Government of the Empire.   After a long conversation on tactical and technical details, we naturally discussed the question that at the time was occupying the minds of most men—the question of how it would be possible to end the War in a reasonable manner. In reply to my question as to how General Ludendorff supposed it would be possible to bring the War to an end, he said :

" For the moment I see no possibility ;   the Entente is now counting on winning the War, and judging by the general position it has the right to do so. Therefore at the present moment we can do nothing. If we succeed in defeating the Rumanians, and in repulsing all the attacks in the West, which unfortunately I can only hope, it will be more possible to talk about peace. And I can give you my word, that if the slightest possibility offers itself of concluding a fairly reasonable peace, I shall grasp it with both hands."

I returned to Brest-Litovsk much calmer.

Meanwhile the campaign in Rumania took its course—with the exception of a few slight frictions —much as the General Headquarters had anticipated.

The appreciation that the General Headquarters had of the co-operation of the Commander-in-Chief in the East in the victorious execution of the Rumanian Campaign found its expression in the following telegram that General Ludendorff addressed to me :

" *December* 12th, 1916.   PLESS.

" COLONEL HOFFMANN, Headquarters East.

" Sincere thanks to you and the members of the Staff for your congratulations. The Victory in Rumania could only have been won as we had gained the battle of the Somme in the West and in the East the tremendous battles on the Southern half of your front, and because we had received from you constant reinforcements at Siebenbürgen in Rumania."

About the turn of the year the German troops approached the Sereth. It was evident that the advance would stop there. In the meantime the Russians had concentrated very considerable forces at the Rumanian frontier. About Christmas, 1916, I wrote a letter to General Ludendorff, in which

I explained that in my opinion the offensive movement in Rumania, that had now become quite a frontal advance, would be entirely stopped about the New Year on the Sereth. If it was desired to continue the campaign, and settle with Rumania definitely, in my opinion there was only one thing to be done, to give up the attacks in the South and to make a thrust from the North. If the General Headquarters was in the position to send the Commander-in-Chief in the East four to six Divisions—it would be simplest to send a part of those already fighting in Rumania—I thought we could accomplish the attack. I proposed that the reinforcements and all the forces the Commander-in-Chief in the East could collect should be concentrated in the neighbourhood of Zloczov. The Russian position was to be broken through there and the offensive was to be continued over Tarnopol along the Great Railway towards Odessa. The bulk of the Russian Army in the Carpathians would by this movement be brought into an untenable position, and I thought that by these operations a great success would be attained. I considered that a break through at Zloczov would be easy to effect and I proposed it should be made exactly as we carried it out in July, 1917.

General Ludendorff replied that he was quite of my opinion with regard to the advance in Rumania which would come to a standstill on the Sereth, as well as with the operations I proposed, which would probably be successful. Unfortunately the preliminary conditions were not obtainable—especially the sending of reinforcements to the Commander-in-Chief in the East. For the moment nothing could be given from the West, and it was impossible to transport troops quickly from Rumania owing to the condition of the Rumanian and Hungarian railways.

I must say a few words about an event that occurred in the Autumn of 1916, and which at the time was generally underrated by most men. I mean the death of the Kaiser Franz Joseph, who closed his eyes on the 21st of November, 1916. He was the last bond that still united the divergent States that formed the Austro-Hungarian Monarchy. His successor, who had been brought up as a simple cavalry officer, and whom the murdered Heir Apparent had purposely prevented from occupying himself with political questions, now found himself facing an impossible task. The worst of it was that the young monarch, encouraged by an ambitious wife whose whole sympathies were on the side of the enemies, and who hated Germany and the Hohenzollerns, and who was surrounded by irresponsible counsellors who flattered his vanity, began by wanting to undertake the leadership both of the political and military events. The first thing he did was to set aside in a somewhat rough manner the Arch-Duke Frederic, who had been till then the Commander-in-Chief of the Army. The Kaiser appointed himself Commander-in-Chief. Although the Arch-Duke Frederic had played no great part, he had given full liberty of action to Conrad von Hötzendorf, the clever Chief of the General Staff, and he had always given him the support of his Imperial name. In all the frictions and differences of opinion that occurred between the Allies, his quiet, amiable and refined demeanour had always acted in a conciliatory manner. One of the first military measure of the new Kaiser was to have the General Headquarters transferred from Teschen to Baden, near Vienna. The Kaiser wanted to get away from the influence of the German General Headquarters in Pless which he found too near. Conrad protested but without success. In this as in every other military or political question, the General gave his opinion in the clear and positive manner he always had done, and in consequence he was obliged to give up his post in the shortest possible space of time. His successor, General von Arz, was a more conciliatory personage, who contented himself with being his Imperial Master's advisory servant, and not what Conrad had been, a responsible Commander-in-Chief.

The position of the Chief of the General Staff degenerated in the hands of its new occupant, especially as he was always obliged to accompany the Kaiser, who constantly travelled about from one part of the front to another, and could never be quiet ; so he, too, could only display his efficiency in travelling about. I had only one opportunity of conversing for some time with the Kaiser Karl. On the occasion of his first visit to the Linsingen Army Group, I had to receive His Majesty, by order of the Commander-in-Chief, who was absent at the time, and in connexion with several inspections I was invited to dinner and passed two hours in the Imperial Court train. The Kaiser, who at that time had not the weary care-worn look he had towards the end of the War, was still fresh and active. He conducted the conversation during these two hours with animation and gave his opinion on military matters by which he displayed his great want of understanding in all he said.

About Christmas, 1916, I found myself obliged to transfer the Administrative Departments of the Commander-in-Chief in the East from Kovno to Bialystock. When I became Chief of this department, I had left this Department as General Ludendorff had organized it. Every fortnight or three weeks the Quartermaster-General came over to Brest-Litovsk, sometimes, if necessary, accompanied by the different Chiefs of departments, to make his report, and to receive my instructions or those of the Commander-in-Chief on any difficult question that might have arisen.

In the autumn of 1916 a certain number of irresponsible people had commenced trying to take away from the Commander-in-Chief in the East the Administrative Department, and to put it under the direct control of the Quartermaster-General. As I did not consider these endeavours practical, but on the contrary I was of the opinion that the Commander-in-Chief in the East must remain complete master of his area, I wrote to General Ludendorff, explained to him my reasons and asked for his decisions. General Ludendorff agreed with me and gave orders that all should remain as heretofore. However I considered the above mentioned change of quarters for the Administrative Department as advisable so as to have it nearer to hand. It was thus possible for the Quartermaster-General, accompanied by the necessary officials from the various Departments, to come to Brest-Litovsk every week to make their reports.

The opinion of the Commander-in-Chief in the East with regard to the Peace Proposals made by the Central Powers in December, 1916, was never asked either officially or privately. He would certainly have been against such a step, which was only calculated to augment the weakness and indecision of those circles which from the very beginning had always been doubtful of the favourable results of the War.

The blunt refusal that the Entente gave to these proposals of the Central Powers, caused us to begin the unrestricted U-boat Warfare on the 1st of February, 1917. I have already given my opinion on the question of the submarine warfare ; I am quite positive first, that Germany had unquestionably every right to carry out an unrestricted U-boat warfare, and secondly, that it was our duty to employ every weapon we possessed to achieve the final victory. It was England who had begun the extension of the War to women, children and non-combatants by the blockade measures she had taken. There can be no doubt we had the right to defend ourselves with similar measures. The outbreak of American indignation against Germany for preventing Americans from coming to England or going in safety anywhere else they desired sounds almost childish. With the same right the Americans might demand that a battle should be broken off, and the artillery fire stopped when a few Americans took it into their heads to go for a walk on that particular battle-field.

Unfortunately by our first attempt at submarine warfare we gave the English the time and opportunity of inventing effective means of opposing it and then we also neglected to employ all our powers in the construction of U-boats.

The assurances of the Admiralty that it would succeed in less than six months in reducing England to submission were, therefore, too optimistic. In

M

order even to form an opinion as to what the causes of this optimism were, and if it was right to run the risk of an American Declaration of War, it would be necessary to have more details than I possess as to what the Navy knew about the enemy's means of resisting this mode of warfare, and why they hoped to attain the desired results in spite of them.

With the decision to commence unrestricted U-boat Warfare the chief centre of the War was temporarily transferred from the land to the sea. On land orders were given to stand on the defensive and await the months required to reduce England to submission with the least possible losses. For these reasons in the West the troops were drawn back from the salient between Arras and Soissons to the so-called Siegfried Line. By this measure it was possible to follow up and retard the enemy's plans of attack and we compelled our adversary to make new and wearisome preparations in order to execute his plan of attack, for which more difficulties were thrown in his way by the entire destruction of all means of communication and all possibility of finding quarters; while on our side, in consequence of the shorter line, we were able to economize in the number of troops required to defend it.

Of course the destructions that this drawing back of our forces rendered necessary, caused shouts of rage in the whole of the enemy Press. However, every expert, even in the adversary's Army will acknowledge that they were quite imperative. I do not doubt for a moment that Englishmen and Frenchmen would have taken the same measures, if the case had been reversed. I need only recall to my memory, at this point, the destruction of the Rumanian petroleum wells wrought by the English.

CHAPTER XIV

PASSING BY THE RUSSIAN REVOLUTION

In the Spring of 1917 the position of the Central Powers was not as threatening as it had appeared at the end of August, 1916. Still it was quite serious enough. The Eastern front was quite secure, but it was impossible to send considerable forces from it to the West, in order to make an offensive attack possible on that front. Owing to the severe fighting on the Somme and at Verdun the West had received a small moral shock ; there was no longer the same confident tone as formerly. The superiority in the quantity of the enemy's war *matériel* was beginning to make itself felt. The deliveries of our industry could not vie with what nearly the whole world brought together against us.

The feeling at home became worse ; the food conditions grew more difficult, the high wages that in accordance with the Hindenburg programme, were being paid to the workmen at home, or to the men who had been discharged and sent home acted depressingly on the Army. There certainly was great injustice in paying high wages to a man who had been recalled from the front because he no longer bore, with his comrades, the hardships and dangers of the trenches, but was at home quietly practising the industry he was used to. Ludendorff's idea when he first introduced the Laws of Compulsory Labour, was evidently that work at home for the War was as much service as military service in the trenches and must be remunerated in the same way. Then America joined the War. And although America had no Army at the time and the Admiralty, in their usual optimistic way of looking at things, declared to everybody that if it was even possible for America to create an Army, she would never be able to transport it to Europe, still there was a large number of earnest people who declared that from the moment America joined the War, all hopes were at an end, that Germany could issue from the struggle victorious.

In March, 1917, at that moment of great difficulty, an event took place affecting the history of the world and which gave Germany once again the possibility of a military victory—this was the beginning of the Russian Revolution. The Tzar had realized that Russia was unable any longer to support the burden of the War, and by continuing it he would expose his State to severe internal convulsions. He was therefore considering the question of a separate peace. In this, however, he calculated without taking into consideration the will of England. The British Ambassador in Petrograd, Sir George Buchanan, had received orders to prevent a Russian separate peace at any price, and he acted in accordance with his instructions when he joined Kerensky and Gutschkov in deposing the Tzar.

It was evident that such an event would produce a great effect on the moral of the Russian Army. The idea naturally occurred that it would be a good thing to accelerate the collapse of the Russian Army by a few strong thrusts on the Eastern front. However, on the one hand the Commander-in-Chief in the East had not the necessary means to do so, and on the other our Foreign Office entertained the delusive hopes of being able to enter into negotiations with the new ruler, Kerensky, which would eventually lead to peace.

Now, when it is possible to examine the conditions more clearly, one is obliged to regret that the first alternative was not adopted, and already in the first days of the Revolution, when the Russian soldier was inclined to draw, what for his understanding, were the natural consequences of the Revolution, that is to say, to lay down his arms and go home, that we did not attempt by a general attack on the whole of the front to cause the Russian soldiers to waver. If we had succeeded in this, no power on earth would have been able to stop the process of disintegration that would then have set in, or to bring the masses again into order.

It is well known that owing to our inactivity Kerensky was able to carry away the Army with his persuasive eloquence and to induce them to continue the struggle and thus to hold eighty German Divisions on the Eastern front during the whole of the Summer of 1917, and to give them work there, too.

In order to encourage the belief in his intentions of concluding a separate peace and to lead our Government further astray, Kerensky ordered his agents abroad to enter into negotiations with the German representatives. As a proof of this I can cite the following fact. About this time I was for one day in Berlin for a business consultation, and while there I received an intimation from the Foreign Office that I was to have an interview with the deputy Erzberger, who was to return that night from Stockholm. I met Herr Erzberger that night and he told me that in Stockholm he had had negotiations with the representative of the Minister-President Kerensky and had nearly succeeded in obtaining the signature to a separate peace with Russia. I was to hold myself in readiness to start with him at a moment's notice for a Peace Conference in Stockholm. I was somewhat sceptical, but of course I could not deny the possibility of such a step. In fact it would have been the most comprehensible thing that Russia could have done, to have concluded a separate peace with Germany. If it had done so then it would have been spared the experience of a Bolshevik Government and the blood of many millions of murdered citizens.

The Commander-in-Chief in the East was, however, not able to abstain entirely from hostilities. Of the two bridgeheads on the Stochod, which the Russians had retained after the hard fighting during the Brussilov offensive, only one, and the smaller one at Witoniec had been recaptured in the Autumn of 1916, while the larger one at Toboly was still in their hands. It formed a constant source of danger for us. In consequence of this the Commander-in-Chief in the East had made preparations already in March to retake it.

The attack was to be made when the thaw would cause inundations in the Stochod lowlands and the bridgehead with its four bridges would be entirely cut off.

The thaw set in early in April and transformed the Stochod lowlands, to the rear of the bridgehead, into a lake about 1,000 metres wide. It would have been a mistake from a military point of view not to take advantage of such a favourable moment for making an attack, as it would be impossible to send reinforcements from the Eastern bank nor could the troops that were stationed at the bridgehead escape our attack. The Commander-in-Chief in the East explained the situation and received permission from the General Headquarters to make the attack.

The attack was executed by the 1st Landwehr Division, under General von Jacoby. Already, several weeks before, the Commander-in-Chief in the East had sent Lieutenant-Colonel Bruchmüller to the Division as Artillery Commander and Adviser. It was only possible to take from the front about 300 guns and 100 Minnewerfer to be held in readiness for this attack. As the number of guns was insufficient to make an attack on the whole bridgehead, it was decided at first to move against only the Southern half ; and then on one of the subsequent days, if possible on the next day, to capture the Northern half.

The attack began at three o'clock on the afternoon of the 3rd of April. Thanks to the admirable directions of Bruchmüller and of the Commander of the Minnewerfer Brigade, Lieutenant-Colonel Henschkel, the effects of the artillery fire were so overpowering that the Russians made scarcely any resistance. The infantry charge that followed immediately after this rain of projectiles surprised most of the Russians in their shelters. After the Southern half of the bridgehead had been captured so quickly and with comparatively so little loss, the attacking party, proceeded, without having orders to do so, to storm the Northern half, and took that too.

The success of the day was astonishingly great as besides quantities of war material we took 10,000 prisoners. Owing to the understanding with the Government that there should not be any important engagements on the Eastern front the Chief Command was quite perplexed how to give an account of these events in the daily Army Report. It was therefore silent about the magnitude of the success. This naturally caused great indignation among the troops that had taken part in the attack and it could not be understood by them, especially as on the following day the Russian Army Report gave an account of the battle in all its details and particulars.

Although at that time the new Russian Rulers showed no signs of having any intention of making peace, but on the contrary, on every possible occasion both Kerensky and the new Minister of Foreign Affairs, Miliukov, reaffirmed their adherence to the alliance with the Entente, and the will to continue the War to a victorious conclusion, the German Government continued to entertain hopes that the Revolution would possibly bring about a separate peace. In accordance with their wish, after the success of Toboly, the General Headquarters forbade the Commander-in-Chief in the East to take any further action for the time.

In February the General Headquarters were removed from Pless to Kreuznach. One of the reasons that induced them to make that change was first, that they expected the Entente's great attack in the West to begin in the middle of February and they wanted to be nearer to the scene of action, and secondly, the chief advantage of Pless, the proximity of the Austrian General Headquarters no longer existed since they had been transferred to Baden, near Vienna.

General Ludendorff ordered me to come to Kreuznach on the 17th of April to make a personal report. I gave him my views on the Russian Army and its fighting strength ; I told him the moral of the army and consequently its fighting power had naturally been much shaken by the Revolution, but that it was impossible to count on seeing it run away before a possible German attack ; on the contrary the Russian Army would be certain to defend itself. The Commander-in-Chief in the East had not, at the time, the reserves necessary for making an attack on a grand scale. If the General Headquarters wished an attack to be made on one, or several points of the Eastern front, in order to make the Russian line give way and cause the disintegration of the Army, they would be obliged to provide their own Divisions for that purpose.

The General Headquarters could not think of doing this at the time, as all the reserves were required in the West. There were no signs of a possible Russian advance to be noticed as yet.

During the rest of our conversation General Ludendorff made no secret of his uneasiness, caused by the internal conditions, and especially by the entire want of decision shown by the Chancellor of the Empire.

Then we spoke of the possibilities there might be in the future, if owing to the Revolution, or to an attack that the German Army made, the Russian lines were broken through, and the Commander-in-Chief in the East were able to send a sufficient number of troops to the Western front, which together with the Western Army, would make a grand offensive thrust on one or other point of the enemy front, and by a successful break through bring about the decisive battle of the campaign.

We were both agreed that every means must be employed to attain this object. In answer to my question of when, and how General Ludendorff proposed to make such an attack, he said that the thrust in the West could not be made as it could in the East. To break through in the West was much more difficult, and it would probably be necessary to try at various points, in order to find out where the enemy was weakest, and at which point an attack should be made with all our strength.

I was not of that opinion, and I told him my mind quite freely. My opinion was, and I have not changed it, that there is only one form of tactics possible, however great or small the fighting power of the combatants may be. If you wish to take upon yourself the difficult decision of making an attack, you must concentrate all the forces you possibly can collect at the point you consider the most favourable for that object. This is naturally a very risky game ; you place all on one card.

At the end of our conversation, which was carried on in the same friendly way as all our previous meetings had been, General Ludendorff pointed out to me there were certain forces at work which were trying to undermine the good understanding that existed between us. I took this news as a joke ; I could not believe such a thing could be possible, as we were both working for the same end with all our strength : for the success of the German arms.

The Commander-in-Chief in the East remained inactive on the Eastern front during May and June.

Already in June signs increased that Kerensky was not in the slightest degree thinking of peace. On the contrary, all the reports that reached us pointed towards Russian preparations for an attack on a large scale. Such preparations could be noticed at Riga, at Dvinsk, at Lake Narocz, at Smorgon, and also along the whole of the Galician front.

It was about this time that Germany had recourse to a new medium of warfare. This was a species of still stronger poison gas—the so-called Yellow Cross. Privy Councillor Haber, to whom we owe the invention of the first poison gas, and who was also the inventor of the Yellow Cross gas, told me after the War that when he had invented the Yellow Cross he went to the General Headquarters and made a report of his invention to General Ludendorff. The difference that existed between the Yellow Cross and the gas that was already in use was that the latter had forced the opponent to use masks, while for the new Yellow Cross, the masks would be of no protection in the long run. The deposits from the Yellow Cross settle on the clothing, eat away the material and cause unpleasant burns. For a time it is possible to find protection from these effects if the soldiers are able often to change their clothes.

In his report to General Ludendorff Privy Councillor Haber suggested that use should be made of the new gas if it was certain that the War could be brought to an end in a year's time. He could guarantee that the enemy would not be able to imitate it in less than a year, so that for a year we would have the possibility of alone being able to use it. If however the War was not finished by the end of a year, Professor Haber thought it would be irretrievably lost for us, if we employed the Yellow Cross in our warfare, as by that time our opponents would have succeeded in imitating it. Thanks to their great industries they would then be able to produce enormous quantities of it and they would in their turn be able to bombard us with it. Protective measures such as mackintoshes, and a change of two or three uniforms, we would be unable to supply as we would not have the necessary materials. Consequently the enemy would not even require to attack ; he would simply bombard us out of each position.

As a matter of fact, Professor Haber made a mistake on one point : our opponents did not succeed in imitating the Yellow Cross in a year but in sixteen months. At the beginning of the Armistice the French alone had 5,000 tons of this gas ready, and to their great sorrow they were unable any longer to employ it against the German troops.

General Ludendorff was therefore running a great risk when he introduced the use of the Yellow Cross ; for although we all hoped that in the course of a year we should be able to defeat Russia and to release from the East the bulk of the German Army for the decisive battle in the West, we could not be sure of it.

We naturally tried, by means of propaganda, to increase the disintegration that the Russian Revolution had introduced into the Army. Some man at home who had connexions with the Russian revolutionaries exiled in Switzerland came upon the idea of employing some of them in order to hasten the undermining and poisoning of the moral of the

Russian Army. He applied to the deputy Erzberger, and the deputy of the German Foreign Office. And thus it came about that Lenin was conveyed through Germany to Petersburg in the manner that afterwards transpired.

I cannot say if the German General Headquarters was cognizant of this measure. The Commander-in-Chief in the East knew nothing about it. We only heard of it months after, when the foreign newspapers began to reproach Germany about it and asserted that we were the fathers of the Russian Revolution. This assertion, which is as false as so much of the enemy propaganda, cannot be denied emphatically enough. As I have already said, the Russian Revolution was brought about by England ; we Germans, who were at war with Russia, had unquestionably the right, when the Russian Revolution did not lead to peace, as at first had been expected, to augment the disorders of the Revolution both in the land and in the Army.

In the same way as I send shells into the enemy trenches, as I discharge poison gas at him, I, as an enemy, have the right to employ the expedient of propaganda against his garrisons. On the other hand, at the same time as Lenin, there appeared in Russia a number of Bolsheviks who until then had lived as political refugees in England and Sweden.

As I have already said, I personally knew nothing of the transport of Lenin through Germany. However, if I had been asked, I would scarcely have made any objections to it, as at that time nobody could foresee the fatal consequences that the appearance of those men would have for Russia and for the whole of Europe.

CHAPTER XV

THE LAST FIGHTS ON THE EASTERN FRONT

THE Commander-in-Chief in the East did not share the hopes of the Foreign Office that a separate peace could be concluded with the Russian Provisional Government. By the end of June the Russian preparations for an attack became more and more apparent, and when the Russian attack began in Galicia on the 1st of July it was no surprise for us. With the recommencement of hostilities by the Russians, the General Headquarters again obtained freedom of action. General Ludendorff telephoned to me, and asked if I still thought it would be possible to break through the Russian line in the direction of Tarnopol, as I had formerly suggested, and by such an action parry the Russian attack. He also asked what reinforcements the Commander-in-Chief in the East would require to do so. I answered joyfully in the affirmative, as a German offensive along the railway line, Lemberg-Tarnopol would necessarily bring the Russian attack that had just begun in Galicia to a standstill. The more forces the Russians concentrated for their attack on the fronts of the Austro-Hungarian Army and the Southern Army, the greater must be our success.

As the lowest possible demand I asked for four Divisions ; the General Headquarters gave us hopes of receiving six.

The Commander-in-Chief in the East began to make energetic preparations for the attack. General von Eben, the leader of the Zloczov sector, was entrusted with the execution of this plan (Major Franz was the Chief of his General Staff). The Artillery preparation was again in the charge of Lieutenant-Colonel Bruchmüller.

The artillery preparation and the bringing up of troops would take about a fortnight, so that we calculated that the 15th of July would be the earliest date for the attack. Already on the 1st of July the Russians began their offensive. The Russians broke into the Austrian positions between Zborov and Brzeczany. By good luck the first troops that had been sent for our attack had already arrived. They were sent at once into action and on the 2nd of July they re-established the position. All the other Russian attacks which were made with great dash, came to grief.

On the 4th of July, strong attacks were made against the Southern Army, which after many days' fighting ended with a complete success for Count Bothmer's Army.

On the 6th and 7th, attacks were begun to the South of the Dniester on the Austro-Hungarian 3rd Army. This army had at last been placed under the Commander-in-Chief in the East. We had placed a German Division at their disposal, and we had intended that this Division should remain as a supernumerary reserve to meet, with a counter attack, any Russian attack that might break through the Austro-Hungarian front, and drive them out again. Only a few days before the attack the Commander-in-Chief had come in person to the Army to assure himself of the condition of the troops and of the positions. He returned quite satisfied with the general position. Unfortunately the Austro-Hungarian Command had not left the German Reserve Division as a supernumerary reserve, but had taken it into action at once, and when the Russian thrust took place on the 6th, there were no troops in reserve and no troops at their disposal to make a counter attack. The German troops were involved in the retreat, the front of the 3rd Army gave way and retired beyond the Lominitza. Kalusz fell into the hands of the Russians. This caused the situation to become very critical. If it were not possible to hold the Lomnitza or to recapture Kalusz, and the retreat of the 3rd Army went still farther back, Stryj, the chief base of the Southern Army, and the oil wells of Drohobicz would be in danger.

The Commander-in-Chief in the East was obliged to support the 3rd Army by sending German troops to them, and the question arose whether it would be possible to make the Zloczov attack on the 15th of July, as had been arranged.

The Bavarian Cavalry Division, that had just arrived, with the Reserve Jager Guard Battalion and the Reserve Guard Schützen Battalion, as well as an Infantry Division were diverted to the 3rd Army. It was also decided for the present to keep to the plans for the attack from Zloczov. If the worst came to the worst, that is, if the German reinforcements were unable to support the 3rd Army, there was always the possibility to march Southwards all the German troops that would have collected by the 15th to the West of our front in the district round Zloczov, and for them to fall on the flank of the Russians who were attacking, from the other side of the Lomnitza.

By the intervention of the Bavarian Cavalry the Russian advance was stopped; the position at Kalusz was re-established, so that the attack from Zloczov could be undertaken. It was a pity we had had to give up some units to the 3rd Army, especially the reinforced Bavarian Cavalry Division. The Commander-in-Chief in the East had planned that a specially equipped Cavalry Corps should be thrown across the Sereth, immediately after the break through from Zloczov had been effected to pursue the retreating Russians East of the Sereth, in a Southern direction. This Corps would probably have had a great success.

The attack had to be postponed for several days because continuous rains that had lasted some days, had rendered the Galician clayey soil quite impossible for any heavy vehicle, except on the high roads. At last, early on the 19th, the advance was able to begin. The chief thrust was led by the 1st and 2nd Guard Infantry Divisions, and the 5th and 6th Infantry Divisions, under General Kathen. Two days before the Commander-in-Chief in the East had come to Zloczov so as to be on the spot to intervene if that were necessary. Thanks to Lieutenant-Colonel Bruchmüller's admirable artillery preparation the break through succeeded perfectly on a width of twenty kilometres. The first day our thrust penetrated to a depth of fifteen kilometres beyond the enemy's line.

Thus, as I have already said, this battle, which in the Reichstag was spoken of as the " tone giving victory," was only fought by chance on the day the Reichstag was sitting.   It is true that during the day General Ludendorff had asked me to give him news of the battle, before six o'clock, the time when the Imperial Chancellor intended to give information about the progress of these operations.

The watch-tower from which the Commander-in-Chief and I watched the fight was connected by telephone with the General Headquarters, so that at five o'clock p.m., the Imperial Chancellor could in a few minutes, through the General Headquarters, be made acquainted with the exact position at the front.

During the next few days the attack went on as it had been planned.   Tarnopol was taken on the 25th, and as it had been foretold the whole of the Russian front, as far as the Carpathians, began to waver. Our nerves were again somewhat overstrained when on the 21st a strong Russian attack at Krevo, South of Smorgon, succeeded in breaking through the front and drove back a Landwehr Division, which, however, fought brilliantly.   For the moment we were unable to help.   A Division that already at the beginning of the Russian retreat, had been found dispensable, was at once ordered to march there, but naturally it would take days before it could arrive.   Until that time, the 10th Army had to help itself, and it was able to do so.   By strong artillery fire, the Russians who had broken into our positions, were held there, and at last they were obliged to give up the captured trenches.   The moral of the Russian Army had suffered greatly by the Revolution.   Earlier our position would have been somewhat worse.

At the beginning of the Russian retreat in Galicia the Allied troops went as far as the Carpathians.

The Southern Army, the Austro-Hungarian 3rd Army and the Austro-Hungarian 7th Army in pursuit of them. In the first days of August the pursuit got as far as Zbrucz, and with the exception of quite small areas the whole of Galicia and the Bukowina were cleared of Russian troops. Unfortunately then the operation stopped. For our German troops the distance from our base was too great, and fresh drafts did not come up. The Austro-Hungarian forces more to the South had not the necessary power of attack to develop the success any further. An attempt of the General Headquarters to improve the success of the Zloczov break through against the Rumanian Army which had been the reason for sending the German Alpine Corps to the Rumanian front as reinforcements, was never carried out, as the Rumanians on their side attacked and had temporarily even local successes.

In the first days of August, when it became clear that before the railways were repaired, a continuation of the pursuit in Galicia was not to be thought of, General Ludendorff called me up. We were both of the opinion that these repairs would require a considerable time, and that it was a pity to leave the troops inactive for so long. General Ludendorff said that with the present development of the position in the West he could not foresee how long he would be able to leave us the Division, that had been sent us as reinforcements for the break through at Zloczov, but on the other hand it was very desirable soon to give the Russians another strong military blow in order to hasten, as much as possible, the disintegration of the Army. He therefore wished to know if I thought, that with the forces that had been placed at our disposal, the old pet idea of the

Commander-in-Chief in the East of a crossing of the Dvina and the capture of Riga would be feasible. If it were, he would try to leave the Division with the Commander-in-Chief in the East for a short time. I naturally affirmed the possibility.

I had already sent for Lieutenant-Colonel Bruchmüller while the operations in Galicia were in progress, and I had ordered him to go to the 8th Army in Mitau and to make the necessary artillery reconnaissances for the crossing of the Dvina at the point that General Otto von Below had suggested to me long ago, and which I myself had reconnoitred at the time.

Unfortunately it took a long time before we could extricate the troops from the Galician front, to get them to the railway and transport them to Mitau. It was only possible to have them ready by the end of August. We passed several days of great suspense, wondering if we would be able to keep the troops or if we would have to give them up before the taking of Riga.

In the West the great battle of Flanders had been raging since the 31st of July, and it was just in the last days of August that there were fierce attacks and serious crises. Twice General Ludendorff telephoned to me that he required the troops, twice that he was still able to do without them. At last we had the certainty that we would be able to keep them, and we began the final preparations for the attack.

The Commander-in-Chief in the East went, as usual, to the scene of action in order to be able, if necessary, to intervene personally. The execution of the attack was entrusted to the 8th Army, under General von Hutier (his Chief of the General Staff was General von Sauberzweig). For this attack three General Commands, 11th Infantry Division and two Cavalry Divisions had been assigned. The real thrust was made by three Divisions—the 19th Reserve Division, 14th Bavarian Infantry Division and 2nd Guard Infantry Division—under the General Command 51. The Commander was General von Berrer, who unfortunately was afterwards killed at Isonzo. After Bruchmüller's 170 batteries and 230 medium and heavy " Minnewerfer " had done their work, the three Divisions that made the thrust were to cross the river at first on pontoons and then on bridges ; each Division was to cross by one bridge.

On the 1st of September, at four a.m., the gassing of the enemy positions began ; after daybreak, at six a.m., the preliminary bombardment ; at nine-ten the first pontoons left the bank. The work of the artillery was again irreproachable. At the beginning of the attack only a few of the enemy guns were fired and this was done badly and irregularly. As soon as the first of the infantry reached the Northern bank the work of putting up the bridges was begun. It was only the bridge situated farthest to the East that received a little enemy fire during its construction and also while the troops were crossing it afterwards, but it caused only slight losses. On the whole the crossing was effected almost in play. The first who crossed the central bridge was H.R.H the Commander-in-Chief, who, as always, felt drawn to the front to accompany the troops in their attack. Our thrust only met with fierce opposition on the Little Jägel, which, however, was soon broken. The results of our thrust in prisoners and booty was smaller than we had expected. Already long before our attack the Russians had evacuated, of their own free will, the Western part of the Riga bridgehead, and they evacuated the remainder with feverish haste when the attack began. I regretted very much that we had not been allowed to make an attack on Riga two years earlier, as the Commander-in-Chief in the East had desired. The Russians would not have evacuated the bridgehead then, and the whole of its large garrison would have fallen into our hands. I have never doubted that at that time the crossing of the river would have been effected quite as successfully as on the 1st of September, 1917, though with somewhat greater losses.

The Army was very enthusiastic and wanted to advance and continue the offensive as far as Petrograd. From a military point of view this would not have been difficult if the General Headquarters could have left us the reinforcements. But this unfortunately was not possible. After a few days the 8th Army had to be stopped in order to send part of the troops to the West, and the greater part to Italy.

The joy with which we were received in Riga itself was quite touching. The inhabitants had suffered very much from the excesses of the troops, whose morale and discipline had sunk very low owing to the Revolution, and also from the hatred of the Letts, and they were thankful to breathe more freely when the German troops occupied the town and brought quiet and order with them.

The Commander-in-Chief in the East had therefore to rely on his own forces for any further development of the operations on the Eastern front. The objectives could therefore only be limited, as the fights at Zloczov and Riga, and especially on the

Little Jägel, had proved that though the Russians had suffered in their morale, and that they had no longer the same power of resistance as formerly, still they would defend themselves. Two small undertakings presented themselves without being sought ; one was the capture of the bridgehead at Jacobstadt where the Russians were still on the South side of the Dvina, the other was the occupation of the islands of Osel, Moon and Dago. The first undertaking was desired by the 8th Army, the second was necessary if we wished to remain in the undisturbed possession of Riga, and it also meant a stronger menace to Petrograd.

For the capture of the bridgehead at Jacobstadt Lieutenant-Colonel Bruchmüller and the necessary amount of artillery was left with the 8th Army. As usual Bruchmüller carried out the placing of his artillery and the preliminary artillery bombardment in a masterly manner and on the 21st of September the bridgehead was easily taken. The preparations for the occupation of the islands required a longer time as the fleet was to take part in it, and naturally it had no experience in the operation of landing troops. On the other hand the leaders of the fleet were pleased, after so long a time, to be able once again to have the opportunity of participating actively in the War otherwise than by the U-boat warfare. The continued inactivity of the High Sea Fleet, the crowding together in one place of such numbers of human material favoured the propaganda of the disaffected elements. Already, for some time past, unsatisfactory reports had been heard about the moral atmosphere in the fleet, especially in connexion with the cases of mutiny that had occurred during the Summer on some of the ships.

The legal inquiry and the discussions in the Reichstag on this subject had caused it to become generally known.

In order to consult about this undertaking I went once to Berlin, and shortly before it began, to Libau. The Commander-in-Chief in the East had entrusted the leadership of this expedition to General von Kathen. He had the 42nd Infantry Division and a Cycle Brigade placed at his disposal.

At the beginning of October the preparations were at last concluded, but unfortunately contrary winds delayed the commencement of the undertaking. It was only on the 11th that the transport flotilla, convoyed by a part of the High Sea Fleet, left the harbour of Libau and landed on the 12th in the Tagger Bay on the Northern side of the island of Osel. The island was well protected by a chain of permanent batteries. The landing, especially on the Northern side, took the Russians by surprise. It was effected without much opposition. The troops that had landed pushed forward rapidly through the island to the South and the East, and by a bold stroke seized the embankment opposite the island of Moon, and the next day they occupied without much resistance the islands of Moon and Dagö.

Afterwards I became very well acquainted with the Russian defender of the island, Admiral Altvater, who belonged to the Bolshevik Armistice Commission, as an expert. He told me at that time the Bolshevik propaganda had permeated so widely among the troops that it was impossible to think any longer of a real defence. The troops simply melted away before his eyes.

While we were gaining easy victories in the East over the Russian Army, which was becoming more and more disorganized, the fierce fights of the battle of Flanders raged in the West, where our troops were only able to maintain their positions with difficulty.

In the Italian theatre of war, since August, attacks were also being made on the Austro-Hungarian Army. In the actions that took place during August and September, and which go under the general name of the 11th Isonzo battle, the Italians had certain successes to the North and the South of Görz. Here also it was very evident that the strength of the Austro-Hungarian troops was exhausted. It might be feared that if there was a 12th Isonza battle they would quite collapse. The German General Headquarters were therefore requested to send them help. Here again the question arose, if the help was to be in the form of a strong thrust which would relieve the Austro-Hungarian Army on the Isonza front, or if we were to begin operations on a large scale in order to give the Italians a destructive blow.

General Ludendorff explains in his book why only the first of these questions could be considered at the time. From these explanations it appears that the General Headquarters had likewise considered the second question, that is, a simultaneous attack from the Tyrol and on the Isonza front. General Ludendorff goes on to say that the only reason against it was that Germany was not able to spare sufficient troops, but only six to eight Divisions which for such a double thrust on a large scale would be insufficient. I am not quite of that opinion. The Eastern front, at that time, would easily have been able to spare strong forces if it had been asked to do so.   It was not to be expected that the Russians would be roused sufficiently to make another attack, so that the risk that was run by even greatly weakening the Eastern front was not very great. If one remembers how small the resisting powers of the Italians were against a German attack it is almost impossible to realize what the success of the larger operation would have been.

CHAPTER XVI

THE ARMISTICE IN THE EAST

In the meantime the destiny of Russia was pursuing its course. The officers were deprived of their rank and discharged. Soldier councils were organized. With this destruction of discipline the Army was done for ; the regiments degenerated into armed hordes which no longer possessed any sort of military value. The ruin of the Army went hand in hand with the internal decomposition. After one unsuccessful attempt, the Bolsheviks succeeded in getting all the power into their own hands. One of the first measures of the new Government was the dispatch of a wireless message on the 26th of November, in which the Commissary Krylenko, who had been promoted from being a corporal to the rank of Commander-in-Chief of the Army, inquired if the German General Headquarters were willing to conclude an Armistice.

General Ludendorff telephoned to me and asked : " Is it possible to negotiate with these people ? " I answered : " Yes, it is possible to negotiate with them. His Excellency requires troops and these are the first that can come."

I have often thought since that it might have been better if the leaders of the German State and Army had refused to have any sort of negotiations with the Bolshevik usurpers. By giving the Bolsheviks the possibility of concluding a peace, and thus satisfying the longing of the people, we also gave them the opportunity of fortifying themselves in power and of retaining it. If Germany had refused to negotiate with them and had demanded representatives of the Russian People and a Government that would have been formed by a free election, the Bolsheviks would not have been able to remain in power. Still, I think, no man of sense will reproach us for having accepted Krylenko's proposal for an armistice.

The General Headquarters accepted Krylenko's proposal and on the 2nd of December the Russian Armistice Delegation crossed our lines at Dvinsk and proceeded to Brest-Litovsk. The Commander-in-Chief in the East received an order to conclude an Armistice. H.R.H. the Commander-in-Chief entrusted me with the direction of the negotiations. A few days before, von Rosenberg, who afterwards became Ambassador, arrived in Brest-Litovsk to represent the German Foreign Office. He had instructions only to be present at the negotiations and to have certain wishes of the Foreign Office taken into consideration. The General Headquarters looked upon the conclusion of an armistice as an entirely military question. Representatives of the Allied Powers also arrived. They were Lieutenant-Colonel Pokorny, for Austria-Hungary; Adjutant-General Zekke represented Turkey, and Colonel Gantschew was sent by Bulgaria.

The conditions that were to be demanded had been settled in principle by the General Headquarters some time before, and they had been sent to the Commander-in-Chief in the East. They were in accordance with the desire to end the War on one front, and they contained no conditions that were unjust or insulting for the Russians. Hostilities were to cease and each side was to retain the positions they held.

On such a basis the conditions of an Armistice could have been settled in a few hours with any normal adversary. With the Russians it was not quite so simple. The Russian Delegation was composed of Joffé, who afterwards unfortunately became so well known to us, Kameneff (Trotski's brother-in-law), Mme. Byzenko, who had already achieved a certain amount of fame through the murder of a Minister, a non-commissioned officer, a sailor, a workman and a peasant. These were the members of the Commission who were entitled to a vote.

Admiral Altvater and a certain number of staff officers were attached to the Commission. They had no vote and had only to act as experts. Karachan was the secretary of the Commission. It was not difficult to house this Commission in some of the huts that we occupied in the Citadel of Brest-Litovsk. With regard to their board, I asked the Commission whether they would prefer to take their meals in the Staff Officers' Mess-room or to have their food sent in to them. The Russians accepted the first proposal. I had one of the large huts arranged for the meetings of the Commission. It was here that we first met the Russian delegates. H.R.H. the Commander-in-Chief greeted them in a speech of welcome and informed them that he was empowered by the Allied Chief Commands to conclude the terms of an Armistice, and that he had appointed me to conduct the negotiations. Joffé replied in a few words.

Then the negotiations began. The first condition

the Russians made was that of entire publicity. They demanded to have the right, at the conclusion of each consultation, to make known by telegraph or wireless the exact text of what each party had said. I had nothing against this ; but in order to avoid the publication of erroneous interpretations on one side or the other, I suggested the appointment of an auxiliary Commission which would draw up the minutes of each meeting immediately after it had taken place, and when these minutes had received the approval of both sides this text would be used for publication. The Russians agreed to this. Then we had to listen to a long propagandistic speech similar to many others we had to hear afterwards from Trotsky. It concluded with a demand to all the powers engaged in the War to end the struggle, to conclude an Armistice, and then settle the terms of a general peace.

My reply to this consisted of the question whether the Russian delegation was authorized by their Allies to make such proposals to us. The military representatives of the quadruple Alliance were present and they were willing to enter into negotiations. The Russians had to confess that they had no such authority. I therefore proposed that they should keep within the limits of the authority they possessed, and that we should proceed to the negotiations of a separate Armistice with Russia.

Other Russian attempts to change the negotiations into propagandistic channels I was also able to check. A little difficulty arose when Admiral Altvater suddenly demanded the evacuation of Riga and of the islands in the Moon Bay. Considering the state of affairs, I felt that this demand was an incomprehensible piece of assurance, and therefore

I refused curtly and energetically to consider it at all. In a pamphlet that one of the Russian experts published afterwards, I saw that all the officers of the General Staff were unanimously against Altvater's idea, as it could not be supposed that we would agree to such a proposal. It was therefore quickly suppressed after my refusal.

The Russians laid great stress on the condition that all the German troops stationed along the Eastern front should remain there, in order to prevent us from transporting them to the West. This demand was easy for us to agree to. Already before the negotiations had begun in Brest-Litovsk the order had been given to send the bulk of the Eastern Army to the Western front. Consequently I was easily able to concede to the Russians, that during the Armistice that was about to be signed, the Germans would not send away any troops from the Eastern front except those that were already being moved, or that had already received orders to go.

Certain difficulties were also caused by the question of the intercourse between the two Armies. With the object of propaganda in view, the Russians naturally laid great store on the most extensive and unhindered intercourse between the trenches, while for us just the contrary was to be desired. I therefore proposed, as it seemed quite impossible to prevent all intercourse, that it was to be limited to certain places. In this way it would be possible to exercise some control, and to intercept the greater part of the propaganda literature that might be expected.

The further demand for the free admission into Germany of all Bolshevik literature and works of enlightenment I was obliged to refuse, but I said

I was quite willing to assist in the export of this literature to France and England.

After much negotiation we at last succeeded in making the draft-treaty for an Armistice which was made out much according to the German plan. Then during lunch Joffé explained, that in order to obtain a power of attorney to sign a definite treaty for an Armistice he must go back to Petrograd. Although this delay was unpleasant for me, I did not share the suspicion of some of the Allies that Joffé's demand was only a manœuvre to break off the negotiations, and that the delegation would probably not return at all. I was not mistaken; however, the delegation returned at the appointed time, and the suspension of hostilities that had been arranged for the time of their absence was changed into an Armistice by the signing of the treaty by both parties.

As the delegates took their meals with us in the mess-room we had the opportunity of getting to know what sort of men some of them were. I had, of course, placed those members of the Commission who had a vote higher than those who were merely experts, so that the workman, the sailor and the non-commissioned officer sat in higher places than the Admiral or the officers. I shall never forget the first dinner we had with the Russians. I sat between Joffé and Sokolnikov, who is now the Commissioner of Finance. Opposite me was the workman, who was evidently caused much trouble by the various implements that he found on the table. He tried to catch the food on his plate first with one thing and then with another; it was only the fork that he used exclusively as a tooth-pick. Almost opposite me sat Frau Byzenko next to

Prince Hohenloke who had on his other side the peasant, a typical Russian figure with long grey curls and an enormous untrimmed beard. He caused a smile to appear on the face of the orderly who was serving round the wine, and had asked him if he would take claret or hock, and he inquired which was the stronger, as he would prefer to have that sort.

Joffé, Kameneff and Sokolnikov all appeared to be extraordinarily intelligent, more especially Joffé. They all spoke enthusiastically of the task that lay before them, the task of leading the Russian proletariat to the heights of happiness and prosperity. They all three did not doubt for a moment that this must happen if the nation governed itself according to the teaching of Marx. The least, that appeared before Joffé's mind's eye, was that all men should be well off, and that a few, among whom, as I gathered, he himself would be numbered, would be a little more than prosperous. To be sure, they all made no secret of the fact that the Russian Revolution was only the first step towards the happiness of all the nations. It was naturally impossible for a State governed on Communistic principles to continue to exist when it was surrounded by States governed by capitalistic systems ; therefore the object they were all striving for was a universal revolution.

It was during these conversations that the first doubts rose to my mind if it had been right for Germany to enter into negotiations with the Bolsheviks at all. They had promised their people peace and happiness. If they were able to take the first home with them, would not their position be greatly strengthened in the eyes of the masses who had longed for peace for many years ? Other doubts came into my mind during the conversations I had with the officers, especially with Admiral Altvater. I talked much with him about the extraordinarily fine Russian Army, and wondered how the Revolution could have so completely corroded it. Altvater replied :

" The influence of Bolshevik propaganda on the masses is enormous. I have already often talked with you about it, and complained that at the time I was defending Osel the troops actually melted away before my eyes. It was the same with the whole Army, and I warn you the same thing will happen in your Army."

I only laughed at the unfortunate Admiral. He was murdered some time after that.

CHAPTER XVII

THE PEACE OF BREST-LITOVSK

THE execution of the terms of the Armistice that had been signed at Brest-Litovsk met with opposition on most parts of the front. It was not that the Russian troops were unwilling to have an Armistice, but because both on the Southern front and in the Caucasus the Bolshevik Delegation was not recognized as possessing the authority to conclude an Armistice. Of all the Commissions that had been appointed to carry out the conditions of the Armistice only one was able to reach its appointed place, and that was in the Northern sector, where it was able to reach Dvinsk. All those that had to go South could not cross the frontier for the time.

The Armistice was concluded with the view of bringing about a peace between Russia on the one side, and the Quadruple Alliance on the other. In order to carry this intention into effect the representatives of the four Powers assembled in Brest-Litovsk. The Secretary of State von Kühlmann came as the representative of the German Empire. By an order of the General Headquarters, I was appointed as their representative to assist the Secretary of State. I was placed under his authority and I had only the right of bringing the wishes, or the opinions of the General Headquarters forward for discussion and, if necessary, to protest against any measures taken by the Secretary of State. I wish this to be well understood, because public opinion is inclined to make the General Headquarters and me, as their representative, responsible for all that took place in Brest-Litovsk and more especially for the Peace that was dictated there. That is wrong. It is Count Hertling, who was at the time Chancellor of the Empire, and the Secretary of State for Foreign Affairs, who are alone responsible for the negotiations and the signing of the Peace that took place.

Count Czernin, a clever, distinguished man, who unfortunately had entirely shattered nerves, came as the representative of the Dual Monarchy. He was firmly convinced that Austria-Hungary would crumble to pieces if they could not obtain Peace very soon. The one thought that completely mastered him was the wish at the very least to come to some arrangement with Russia and to be able to take a Treaty of Peace home with him.

The Bulgarian mission was headed by their minister Popoff, an unimportant personage, with a limited political horizon and, perhaps, just in consequence of this, great obstinacy. The clever Minister President Radoslavor and the Turkish Grand Vizier Talaat only appeared on the scenes later.

The representatives of Turkey were at first the Ambassador in Berlin, and former Grand Vizier, Hakki, an unusually clever and skilful diplomatist and the Secretary of State for Foreign Affairs, Messimy Bey.

The leaders of the Russian delegation were at first : Joffé, Kameneff and Professor Pokrovsky.

To house and feed these numerous missions

(they numbered together about four hundred people) was naturally no easy matter. However, thanks to the ability of the Quartermaster-General and of the managers of the various officers' messes, these difficulties were mastered. In the former Russian theatre, which had almost escaped destruction, a hall of sufficiently large dimensions was prepared for the general meetings ; while for the smaller assemblies the smaller room we had used for the negotiations of the Armistice was at our disposal.

Shortly after the arrival of Kühlmann and Czernin, I was called upon to be present at a consultation that took place between them for the settlement of the first steps that were to be taken. The first thing that had to be done was to send the Russians an answer to their Peace proposals, which, like the proposals they had sent about making an Armistice, were addressed to all the belligerents and suggested that all should meet at a round table to negotiate the terms for putting an end to the fighting. The Russian proposals spoke of a Peace without annexations.

Secretary of State von Kühlmann's standpoint was that Germany would accept this proposal if the Russians were able to induce the Entente States to agree to such negotiations. In his opinion the settlement of the question of the Border States : Poland, Lithuania, and Kurland, did not come into the category of annexations as the legally appointed representatives of these States had decided of their own free will, a long time previously, to separate themselves from Russia and to place the settlement of their future status in the hands of Germany or the Central Powers. Count Czernin was naturally anxious to accept the proposal of a

Peace without annexations, and he certainly ought to have been pleased to enter into negotiations on such a basis with the enemy Powers, who had decided on the partition of Austria-Hungary.

The two statesmen had decided to send an answer that agreed without any restrictions to a Peace without annexations if " the Entente Powers would also agree to negotiate a Peace on similar terms." I did not like this answer. First, because by adopting the Russian style, it contained a number of expressions that went against my feelings ; and secondly, because at bottom it was a lie. It was entirely based on the conditional phrase : " If the Entente," etc. I considered it would have been more correct to have kept strictly to facts by answering the Russians that the Central Powers were willing to enter on negotiations for a general Peace, as they had proved by several proposals they had already made, and by the resolutions of the German Reichstag, but as the Russian Peace Delegation had no legal right to speak for the other Powers of the Entente, and until the Russians were able to produce credentials that would entitle them to do so, it would only be possible for them to negotiate a separate Peace with the Quadruple Alliance.

I mentioned my scruples to the Secretary of State. He, however, stuck to his decision. As he had gone with the Chancellor of State to the General Headquarters before coming to Brest-Litovsk, I had to suppose that during the consultation of the Highest Leaders of the State with the Highest Leaders of the Army, a decision had been arrived at with regard to the *modus procedendi*, so I had to submit.

When it came to the signing of the answer to the

Russians, the Bulgarians made difficulties. Minister Popoff declared that they—the Bulgarians—had been promised certain portions of Serbia and the Dobrudja, and they could not think of endangering these promised territories by putting their signature to such an answer. They had entered into the War with the object of annexations and they had no intentions of resigning them. It was in vain that Kühlmann and Czernin lavished their persuasive eloquence on Popoff ; even when they had explained to him a hundred times that there was no danger, that it was only done to make a good impression at the very beginning of the negotiations, that it was impossible to suppose England and France would agree to enter into negotiations of Peace, and that all the explanations that the Central Powers were giving now would be invalid if the Entente were not ready to negotiate—still he obstinately stuck to his " No."

General Gantscheff, the second Bulgarian representative, showed himself more amenable and more sensitive to this diplomatic logic. He sent a detailed telegram to Tzar Ferdinand and he was able to obtain from him an order for Popoff to sign. Messimy Bey was also in doubt about signing, but he was more easily persuaded by Kühlmann and Czernin than the Bulgarian could be. On the 24th of December the answer was delivered to the Russians. Some expressions in this note, that appeared to me too humiliating, I had succeeded in having deleted or altered.

The Russians were triumphant and telegraphed their satisfaction to Petrograd. By mutual consent we had now to wait ten days, to give the Entente time to notify if they wished to participate in the Peace Conference.

Secretary of State Kühlmann and Count Czernin suggested to the Russians not to remain inactive during these ten days, but to organize a number of Commissions and to proceed at once to the settlement of various secondary points of the Treaty of Peace. The Russians agreed to this. Joffé and some of the members of the Delegation had the intention of again returning to Petrograd during that time. He hinted that when he came back he would probably be accompanied by the Commissioner for Foreign Affairs, Trotsky.

From the conversations we had I received the impression that the Russians had misunderstood the offer of our diplomatists, and that they supposed a Peace without annexations would give them back the Polish, Lithunanian and Kurland Governments. My impression was confirmed by a conversation Major Brinckmann had with the Russian Lieutenant-Colonel Fokke. Fokke said quite positively that immediately after Peace had been signed the German troops would retire beyond the old frontier of 1914. I told the Secretary of State that I considered it impossible to allow the Russians to go back to Petrograd under such misapprehensions. If in Petrograd they not only led their Government, but also large circles of the people, to believe that the Peace they were about to sign would guarantee to Russia the old frontiers of 1914, the admission that their comprehension of it had been a false one and that the Note of the Central Powers must be understood differently, in other words that they had been deceived, could only result in frantic indignation on the Russian side. I therefore considered it was quite time to undeceive them on this point and I offered to do so.

The Secretary of State saw that I was right, and agreed with me. Count Czernin agreed, too.

That morning during lunch I said to Joffé, who sat next to me, I perceived that the Russian Delegation had understood the meaning of a Peace without forcible annexations differently to the meaning attached to it by the representatives of the Central Powers. The latter took up the standpoint that it was not a forcible annexation if portions of the former Russian Empire decided, of their own free will, and by a determination of their existing political representatives, on a separation from the Union of Russian States, and on being united to the German Empire or any other State. The Russian rulers themselves had given these rights to the different States by their declaration of the Self-determination of Nations. This applied to the positions of Poland, Lithuania and Kurland. The representatives of the three States had announced their withdrawal from the Union of Russian States. The Central Powers did not consider it an annexation if the future fate of these States were decided by a direct understanding with their representatives, and with the exclusion of the Russian State.

Joffé looked as if he had received a blow on the head. After lunch we had a conference that lasted several hours. The Russians were represented by Joffé, Kameneff and Pokrovsky—the Germans by the Secretary of State, Czernin and myself. In this conference the Russians gave free vent to their disappointment and indignation. Pokrovsky said, with tears in his eyes, it was impossible to speak of a Peace without annexations when about eighteen Governments were torn from the Russian Empire. In the end the Russians threatened to break off the conference and depart.   Count Czernin was beside himself.   He had brought with him instructions from the Kaiser not to allow the Conference of Brest to fail on any account, and if the worst came to the worst, and the German demands endangered its continuation, he was even to make a separate Peace with the Russians.   His nerves completely gave way, and he not only spoke very excitedly with the Secretary of State of his intentions of making a separate Peace, but he also sent his military adviser, Lieutenant Field-Marshal Csicsericz, to my office, to threaten me in the same manner, evidently hoping to make an impression on the German Headquarters in this way.   I could not understand the Count's excitement.   In my opinion there was no question of the negotiations being broken off by the Russians. The Russian masses were longing for peace, the Army had crumbled away, it consisted now of mere insubordinate armed hordes, and the only possibility for the Bolsheviks to remain in power was by signing a Peace.   They were obliged to accept the conditions of the Central Powers, however hard they might be.

I therefore answered Lieutenant Field-Marshal Csicsericz's threat of a separate peace very calmly ; that I thought this a brilliant idea, as it would free for us the twenty-five Divisions that till then I had been obliged to keep on the Austrian-Hungarian front, for the support of their Army.   By a separate Peace the right wing of the German Army would be automatically covered by Austria-Hungary, so that the military position of the German Eastern Army would derive special benefit by such a measure.

Secretary of State Kühlmann also received Czernin's threat of a separate peace with great calmness.

He told me that he had requested a written statement of the standpoint of the Austro-Hungarian Government, and it appeared to me that he was not loath to have in his hands such a proof if the wishes of the General Headquarters went too far. The excited discussions, and the still more excited exchange of telegrams of these days had at first no results as we were obliged to wait quietly to see if the Russian Delegation would return from Petrograd or if it would not return, though only one of us all who feared this was Count Czernin.

During this pause Count Czernin went to Vienna and Secretary of State Kühlmann to Berlin, and by his request I accompanied him.

When I was announced to General Ludendorff I was received very coldly and with the angry question :

" How could you allow such a Note to be dispatched ? "

I explained that I had supposed, and I was bound to suppose, that the general outline of the negotiations had been discussed and settled between the General Headquarters and the Chancellor of the Empire and the Secretary of State during their conferences in Kreuznach. General Ludendorff denied this, but admitted that I had the right to suppose this had been done.

Even now it is a mystery to me that the General Headquarters and the leaders of the Government had not arrived at an understanding of such a nature during the conference they had had on the 18th of December. It is impossible to settle the lines for so difficult a task as a Treaty of Peace by making all sorts of general conversation on both sides.

In connexion with my conversation with General Ludendorff I had to report myself to the Kaiser in the Bellevue Palace. His Majesty took great interest, both in the Armistice, which had been concluded, and in the negotiations that were in progress. I had to describe to him minutely all that had occurred and the personalities of all who had taken part in the negotiations, and as my report was not finished when the lunch hour approached, I was bidden to lunch. After the meal His Majesty continued the conversation on the question of the Eastern front and alluded to the Polish difficulties. He demanded my opinion on the Polish question. I hesitated a little and begged His Majesty to excuse me from giving it, as my opinion differed from the views of the General Headquarters and I did not wish to put myself in opposition to them. His Majesty replied :

" When your Chief War Lord wishes to hear your opinions on any subject, it is your duty to communicate them to him quite irrespective of their coinciding with the opinions of the General Headquarters or not."

I was an enemy of any settlement of the Polish question which would increase in Germany the number of subjects of Polish nationality. Notwithstanding the measures that Prussia had taken during many decades, we had not been able to manage the Poles we have, and I could not see the advantage of any addition to the number of citizens of that nationality. To add to Germany a broad strip of border-land with a population of about two million Poles, as the General Headquarters demanded would, in my opinion, only be a disadvantage to the Empire. I considered the so-called Germano-

Polish settlement as still worse. In my opinion, the new Polish frontier ought to be drawn in such a way that it should bring to the Empire the smallest possible number of Polish subjects and that there should be only a few unimportant corrections of the frontier. To the latter I reckoned a small strip of land near Berdzin and Thorn, so that in any subsequent war the enemy artillery would not be able to fire straight into the Upper Silesian coal mines or on to the chief railway station of Thorn. I also calculated on the heights of Mlawa for the better defence of the Soldau district, and lastly, the crossing of the Bobr, near Osovice, which had caused us so many headaches.

The increase in Polish inhabitants, which would amount to about 100,000, would have to be taken into the bargain. But beyond that not a man.

During this conversation His Majesty agreed with me.

On the 2nd of January there was a consultation between the Government and the General Head-quarters in the General Staff and afterwards a Privy Council in the Bellevue Palace. I was ordered to attend both. I tried in vain to see General Luden-dorff for a moment previously, to inform him of the report His Majesty had demanded of me.

At the Privy Council the first subject of discussion was the progress of the negotiations in Brest-Litovsk. Secretary of State von Kühlmann made a statement of what had been done as yet, and how he expected the further progress of the negotiations would be, to which His Majesty assented. Then the Kaiser began to speak on the Polish question. He had had the new Polish frontier drawn on a map in accor-dance with my report, and said that he considered this the right one. He could not refuse to take into consideration the serious objections there were to the settlement proposed by the General Head-quarters and which, on his demand, had been laid before him by me, in consequence of which he must retract the consent he had previously given to the project of the General Headquarters. General Lu-dendorff contradicted these objections in a somewhat vehement manner. His Majesty's decision could not be definitely given at once and he earnestly entreated that the General Headquarters might be permitted to lay the case again before His Majesty. General Field-Marshal von Hindenburg seconded this request. His Majesty brought the somewhat painful scene to an end by saying :

" I therefore await a further report from the General Headquarters."

The Privy Council had not settled anything definitely or decidedly. The Secretary of State had not been told quite clearly what position he was to take up at Brest, nor had the Polish question been decided. His Majesty the Kaiser had only approved of what Kühlmann had done so far, and he had authorized him to continue on the same path. The difficult problem of the Border States remained unsettled. It is true the General Headquarters had advised a more rapid and energetic manner of carrying on the negotiations at Brest, by which the fate of the Border States that were already in the possession of Germany would be settled by their being definitely separated from Russia and awarded to the Central Powers. However, the Secretary of State Kühlmann had been successful in carrying his point of trying to have the separation of the Border States not made by the way of annexation but by the more amicable way of the Right of Self-determination of the Peoples. After this meeting, on the evening of the 2nd of January, we started again for Brest-Litovsk.

It was quite clear to me that General Ludendorff would be very much offended with me for differing so completely from them on the Polish question, and I had not deceived myself. Already the next day I was telephoned to from Berlin, and informed that Hindenburg and Ludendorff had made a cabinet question of the case. They both threatened to resign and demanded that I should be recalled. The Kaiser gave in on the Polish question but refused to alter the personal one. He protected me, as might have been expected.

Besides these facts which were only told me, I felt the resentment of the General Headquarters personally in a series of orders and questions that were sent me in a form which showed me great men can also be very small sometimes.

At the end of the first week in January the Russians returned from Petrograd. I had never doubted that they would do so. The former leader, Joffé, returned, but not as the head of the deputation ; his place was taken by Trotsky. There were two versions of the reason for this change : one report said Trotsky had been furious that Joffé had not seen at once the craftiness of the Central Powers' answer and that this was the cause of his being superseded ; he was only retained in the delegation on account of his local and personal knowledge of Brest-Litovsk and its inhabitants, which he had acquired during the weeks he had been there and which the delegation wanted to utilize. The other version said that Joffé had really been enraged at the hypocritical offer of Peace made by the Central Powers and that he had refused to continue the negotiations. It was against his will and only at Trotsky's request that he had given in, and had consented to accompany the delegation and assist it with his personal knowledge.

Trotsky was certainly the most interesting personality in the new Russian Government : clever, versatile, cultured, possessing great energy, power of work, and eloquence, he gave the impression of a man who knew exactly what he wanted and who would not be deterred from using any means for the attainment of his end. The question has been much discussed whether he came with the intention of concluding a peace, or if from the very beginning he only wanted to find the most visible platform from which to propagandize his Bolshevik theories. Although propaganda played such a prominent part in the whole of the negotiations of the following weeks, I still think that Trotsky at first wanted to try to make peace and that it was only afterwards, when he had been driven into a corner by Kühlmann's dialectics, for which he was no match, that he thought of bringing the conference to a spectacular finish by declaring that, though Russia could not accept the conditions of peace offered by the Central Powers, nor even fully discuss them, still, it declared the War to be finished.

Even before the negotiations had begun a new group of participants presented themselves in Brest-Litovsk. They were the representatives of the Ukrainian Peasant States, whom the Rada had sent in order to make a separate peace for the Ukraine, basing their demand on the declaration of the Petrograd Soviet Government regarding the Self-Deter-

mination of the Peoples. Secretary of State Kühlmann and I received the Ukrainians with pleasure,
as their appearance offered a possibility of playing
them off against the Petrograd delegation. To
Count Czernin, however, their arrival only caused a
new trouble, as it could be foreseen that the representatives of the Ukraine would make demands
about the political rights of their fellow countrymen
who were living in the Bukovina and East Galicia.

With Trotsky's arrival the unconstrained intercourse that had existed until then outside the
meeting-hall came to an end. Trotsky requested
that the Delegation might have their meals in their
quarters, and prohibited all private intercourse and
all conversations.

At the very beginning of the negotiations there
was a slight collision. Mr. Trotsky seemed to consider the platform in Brest-Litovsk not large enough
for his propagandistic designs. He demanded that
the scene of the negotiations should be removed to
Stockholm. His chief object in this demand was
the wish to get away from Brest-Litovsk, the Military
Headquarters in the War zone, where it would be
impossible to get into direct contact with the dissatisfied elements of the Central Powers, with whose
help the inflammatory portions of his speeches
would be underlined and carried to wide circles of
the people for propaganda purposes. Naturally
the Central Powers refused this demand. Then
the battle of words began between Trotsky and
Kühlmann that lasted several weeks, and led to
nothing. It was only gradually that it became
clear to all the parties concerned in the negotiations
that the chief object Trotsky was pursuing was to
preach the Bolshevik doctrines, that he was only

speaking to the gallery and did not set the slightest store by any practical work that was to be done. Simultaneously with his speeches wireless messages were sent to " all," inciting to revolt, to disobedience, to the murder of the officers. I protested energetically against this ; Trotsky promised to desist, but the instigating wireless messages continued to be sent. The negotiations went farther and farther from their real object and turned into theoretical discussions. Trotsky's tone became with each day more aggressive. One day I therefore pointed out to Secretary of State Kühlmann and Count Czernin that it was impossible to attain our object in this way ; that it was absolutely necessary to bring the negotiations back to a basis of facts, and offered at the next opportunity to represent to the Russians how the position really was, and why we were assembled there. As always the Secretary of State was quite of my opinion. Count Czernin, whose nerves became worse every day, as he felt that he never came an inch nearer his object of returning to Vienna with a Treaty of Peace, had some objections to make, as he still hoped by amiability and diplomatic cleverness to get round the Bolshevik gentlemen. At last he also gave in. It was decided that at the next favourable opportunity Secretary of State Kühlmann would pass the word on to me, and I should say whatever I thought necessary.

The opportunity came sooner than we had expected. Already the next day Kameneff, Trotsky's brother-in-law, made a speech by Trotsky's order, which made the blood of all the officers who were present rise to their heads. It was wonderfully audacious ; the Russians might have had a certain right to speak in that way if the positions had been reversed, that is to say, if the German Army had been defeated and lay defenceless on the ground, and the Russian Armies had been victoriously in possession of German territory.

A glance at the Secretary of State showed me that his patience was also exhausted. He desired me to speak, and I explained to the Russians on the one side the exact position, and on the other side, the difference there was between their words and their deeds, how they made great speeches about freedom of conscience and freedom of words, self-determination of the peoples, and other beautiful things, and how in fact they permitted no sort of freedom in the spheres under their power. How they had dispersed with bayonets the Constitutional Assemblies that went against them, how they had expelled by force of arms the National Assembly of the White Russians in Minsk, in the same way as they had now turned out the freely elected Rada of the Ukrainians. The question of the Border States was settled for the German General Headquarters. They took up the standpoint that the legal representatives of these States had decided on separating from Soviet Russia, and that no further vote was necessary. I spoke seated and absolutely quietly ; I neither raised my voice in any way, nor did I thump with my fist on the table as reports had it.[1]

When I finished there was profound silence. Even Mr. Trotsky, at the first moment, could not find a word in reply. It was difficult to find anything to say against it, as all I had asserted was in strict

[1] Compare my description with the report given by Karl Friedrich Nowak in his book, *The Collapse of the Central Powers* (Chapter : " Brest-Litovsk ") which was written from details given by those who were present and is quite truthful on every point.

accordance with facts. The meeting was quickly adjourned.

The actual effects of my explanations were not as great as I had expected. At the next meeting Trotsky confined himself to saying a few meaningless words of defence and immolated my speech as a simple expression of military propaganda. After this he still avoided touching on any grounds that might have led to practical work, and continued his dialectic fireworks. Unfortunately the Secretary of State also failed to take advantage of the position created by my speech to force the meetings to begin practical work.

Through the Chief of the Operations Department I had had my motives in making that speech explained to General Ludendorff and I had begged him to give me his opinion on it. General Ludendorff approved of my action, and encouraged me to do all I could to shorten the negotiations and bring them down to realities. Not having been able to attain any real advance by my interruption of Trotsky's flow of eloquence, another way was open to me : this was the negotiations with the Ukrainian Delegation.

The Ukrainian representatives did not hold themselves aloof from us as Trotsky did. They had their meals with us in the officers' mess-room, and they conversed with us quietly about their objects and their wishes. I had the impression that we would soon be able to come to terms with them. I therefore offered Count Czernin, who was naturally the most important personage in these negotiations with the Ukrainians my services as intermediary. In this I acted in accordance with the opinion I held that the conclusion of a separate peace between the Central Powers and the Ukraine would naturally also force Trotsky to emerge from his reserve. The young representatives of the Kiev Central Rada were not sympathetic to Count Czernin and he did not like to negotiate with young Messrs. Liubinsky and Sevruk, who were scarcely past their student years, on a footing of equality. I proposed that the Count should authorize me, first to find out privately from the Ukrainians under what conditions they would be willing to conclude a separate peace with the Central Powers. Count Czernin gave me this authority. After a certain amount of persuasion on my part the two Ukrainian gentlemen at last divulged their wishes. They extended to the annexation by the Ukraine of the districts round Cholm, and also the Ruthenian portions of East Galicia and the Bukovina.

As I considered an independent Polish State to be a Utopia, and I still hold that opinion, I had no hesitation in promising the Ukrainians my support with regard to the Cholm lands. On the other hand, I looked upon the demand for Austrian-Hungarian territory as a piece of impudence and I gave the two young men to understand as much, in a somewhat rough manner. They had evidently expected my reply, as they assured me most amiably that they would require to obtain new instructions from Kiev to be able to continue negotiations on the basis produced by our conversation.

Count Czernin's position became very difficult about this time owing to a food catastrophe that broke out in Vienna in consequence of the want of foresight of the Austro-Hungarian Government. In order to prevent a state of famine Berlin had to be asked for aid. Notwithstanding its own want,

Berlin assisted but in consequence Count Czernin naturally was deprived of the possibility of threatening to conclude a separate peace with Trotsky, or even to try to do so. On the other hand the separate peace with the Ukraine which I had looked upon as a measure that might force Trotsky to sign a peace, now became, as a means of obtaining bread, a vital necessity for Count Czernin. It was a bad thing for Austria that it was impossible to hide her desperate position from the Ukrianians.

In the meantime their new instructions had arrived from Kiev, and they were submitted to me at another consultation. The Cholm district was *conditio sine qua non*. It apparently had dawned upon the Rulers in Kiev that the defeated side could not demand the cession of territory from the other party. They therefore renounced all claim to any part of East Galicia and the Bukovina, but they demanded that these districts should be formed into independent Austro-Hungarian Crownlands under the Habsburgers. I had the impression that the Ukrainians would not recede from these conditions, and that the critical position of Count Czernin was well known to them. Czernin's difficulties were twofold : if he consented to the cession of the Cholm district to the Ukraine, he was threatened with the deadly hatred of the Poles ; if he agreed to the creation of Ruthenian Crownlands he introduced the question of Self-determination into the mixed nationalities of the Austro-Hungarian Empire, while on the other hand, the cession of the Cholm district without consulting the population was in exact opposition to the principles of Self-determination.

Czernin's indisposition entailed a pause of two

days, after which he authorized me to continue negotiations with the Ukrainians on the basis of their demands and, if possible, come to a settlement with them.

In the meantime the negotiations with Trotsky went on in the same aimless manner.

Apparently the Russian Commissar of the People realized the danger with which he was threatened by our negotiations for a separate peace with the Ukraine, for suddenly he asserted that the Ukrainian representatives, whom till then he had recognized, had not the right to carry on a separate negotiation in the name of the Ukraine, as the frontiers between Soviet Russia and the Ukraine had not been fixed as yet. On this question and some others he must consult the Petrograd Government. He proposed to have again an interruption of a few days in the negotiations, as he was obliged to go to Petrograd.

Of course this was not the reason for his journey to Petrograd. I concluded that he wanted to convince himself how far the Bolshevik rule had become stabilized in Petrograd, if in consideration of the wishes of the people he would have to conclude a real peace with the Central Powers, or if he could bring the negotiations to an end with the spectacular effect he afterwards had recourse to. Secretary of State Kühlmann went to Berlin to render an account of the negotiations to the Reichstag and Count Czernin went to Vienna in order to obtain sanction for the conditions of peace with the Ukraine.

After the return of all the delegates, in the early days of February, Trotsky tried to prevent the separate Peace with the Ukraine in another way. He brought two Ukrainians with him, Medvediev and Shakhrei, who were sent not by the Central Rada, but by a new Bolshevik opposition government that had been formed in Kharkov. The representatives from the Central Rada protested against this attempt at checkmate, and it came to lively encounters between the Ukrainian and the Russian delegates. In an excellent speech Liubinski laid before the Bolsheviks the whole list of their sins. In his answer Trotsky contented himself with hinting that the power of the Central Rada had vanished and that its representatives could look upon their room in Brest-Litovsk as the only space of which they had any right to dispose.

Judging by the reports from the Ukraine that I had before me, Trotsky's words seemed unfortunately not to be without foundation. Bolshevisim was advancing victoriously, the Central Rada and the Ukrainian provisional government had fled. Secretary of State Kühlmann and Count Czernin decided, however, despite these transitory difficulties for the Ukrainian government to adhere to the arrangements. The difficulties were transitory in so far as at any time we could support the government with arms and establish it again. They therefore refused to recognize the Ukrainian representatives whom Trotsky presented on the grounds that in the beginning of January, Trotsky himself had recognized the Ukrainian delegation as the representatives of the people.

During those days I often admired the young Ukrainians. It is certain that they knew that the possible help from Germany was their last hope, that their government was but a fictitious conception ; nevertheless, they held to the demands they had succeeded in obtaining and they did not give way a finger's breadth in all their negotiations with Count Czernin.

The Peace with the Ukraine was signed. It was a hard blow for Trotsky, as it was clear that now the negotiations with him must be brought to some sort of conclusion.

In the meantime, despite my protest and notwithstanding all Trotsky's assurances, the propagandistic appeals " to all " and more especially to the troops were despatched as usual. It was at this time that an appeal was addressed to the troops in which they were summoned to murder their officers. Until now only the General Headquarters had urged that a decision should be arrived at with Trotsky but after this the Secretary of State, von Kühlmann, received a telegram from His Majesty instructing him to send an ultimatum to Trotsky demanding a settlement within twenty-four hours. But just at that moment the Secretary of State, von Kühlmann had the impression that it might be possible to bring Trotsky to a settlement of the negotiations, as Trotsky, probably under the impression that the Peace with the Ukraine had, for the first time, approached the question of peace from a practical point. He had sent to ask the Secretary of State if it would not be possible, by some means, to arrange that Riga and the Islands that lay before it should be retained by the Russian Empire.

The Secretary of State was in a difficult position. He did not hesitate for a moment to sacrifice himself for what he thought right ; he telegraphed in reply that the moment was ill-chosen to send an Ultimatum of such short respite and that he earnestly advised that it should not be presented. If His

Majesty insisted on its delivery, the Government would have to find another Secretary of State. He would await an answer until four-thirty that afternoon ; if by that time no further orders about the Ultimatum were received, he would pass on to the order of the day. Nothing occurred until four-thirty and Kühlmann kept the order for an Ultimatum in his pocket. He had tried to nail Trotsky down with this Riga proposal. He had sent the Ambassador von Rosenberg to Trotsky to tell him that if he sent in a written offer of peace on the condition of Riga and the Islands remaining Russian it would be possible to discuss the question. After some hesitation Trotsky refused to comply with this demand. On the other hand he perceived that he could no longer go on simply making speeches and proposals, and that the Central Powers would now demand acts. He evidently also thought that he had produced sufficient effect with his propaganda, and now sought for an opening which would enable him to bring the Brest negotiations to an end in a way that would produce the greatest possible effect. In the meeting of the 10th of February he announced, that although he would sign no Treaty of Peace, Russia would consider the War at an end from that time, she would send all her Armies to their homes and that she would proclaim the fact to all the Peoples and all the States.

The whole congress sat speechless when Trotsky had finished his declaration. We were all dumbfounded. That same evening the Austro-Hungarian and the German diplomatists had a meeting to consult on the new position at which I was also summoned to assist. The diplomatists of both countries were unanimous in asserting that they would accept this declaration. As although no Peace had been signed the conditions of peace were established between the two countries by this declaration. I was the only one against it. We had made an Armistice with the Russians with the object of arranging the terms of peace. If peace were not concluded the object of the armistice was not attained, and, therefore, the armistice came automatically to an end, and hostilities must recommence. Trotsky's declaration was, in my opinion, nothing more than a denouncement of the Armistice.

I was unable to bring the diplomatists round to my opinion. One of Czernin's assistants, the Ambassador von Wiesner, quite misunderstanding the situation in the manner this diplomatist was wont to distinguish himself, had already telegraphed to Vienna that Peace was concluded with Russia. I apprised the General Headquarters of the results of these conversations and received a reply that the High Command was quite of my opinion. It is well known that the High Command of the Army was also able to persuade the Government and the Foreign Office to accept their point of view.

On the eighth day after the negotiations had been broken off so abruptly by Trotsky, the Eastern Army resumed the offensive. The demoralized Russian troops offered no kind of resistance, if it were possible even to call them troops, as it was only the staffs that still remained ; the bulk of the troops had already gone home. We simply swept over the whole of Livonia and Esthonia, and took possession of them. Our troops were greeted everywhere as deliverers from the Bolshevik terror, and not only by the Baltic Germans, but likewise by the Letts and Esthonians.

Two days after our advance had recommenced a wireless message was received from Petrograd announcing that the Russians were ready to renew the negotiations and conclude a Peace and also begging that the German advance might be stopped. It had very quickly been proved that Trotsky's theories could not resist facts. The German Army advanced only as far as Lake Peipus and Narva, in order to release at least all the Baltic members of our race from the Bolsheviks and all their crimes. Then the advance was stopped and the Bolsheviks were informed that they might send a delegation, authorized to sign a Peace, to Brest-Litovsk. Almost immediately the delegation under the leadership of Sokolnikov, arrived. The representatives of the Quadruple Alliance, who had dispersed to all the points of the compass, also hastened back. But in the same manner as on the Russian side, so also on our side there appeared, one may say, only the second fiddles. Kühlmann, Czernin, Talaat, Rodoslavov, had gone in the meantime to Bukharest for the opening of the Peace Conference with Rumania and did not return, but sent their representatives. The Ambassador, von Rosenberg, came as the representative of Germany.

This time also the negotiations were carried on in a very extraordinary manner. At the first meeting von Rosenberg proposed to discuss at once each of the paragraphs of the draft of a Treaty of Peace he had brought with him ; Sokolnikov replied to this proposal with a request that the whole draft might be read out to him. When it had been read to him, he said that he did not demand the discussion of the single points, and that the Russians were willing to sign the draft that had been presented to them. The only reason such a proceeding could have had was the intention to prove more completely that they were forced into signing a peace that was dictated to them. As propaganda has often asserted that I was the author of this " Peace of Violence," I wish again to state emphatically that I had not the slightest influence on the drafting of this Treaty of Peace ; I became acquainted with its contents, for the first time, when it was publicly read aloud in the presence of the Russian Delegation. The definite acceptance of it by Sokolnokov took place at a private meeting of the diplomats at which I was not even present.

Of course the greatest propaganda with this " Peace of Violence " was made by the Entente. I would only ask the Entente why they did not change this treaty when they had won the War and completely changed the political conditions of Europe by the peace they dictated ? The Peace of Brest-Litovsk was declared as annulled, but its chief conditions remained unchanged. It never occurred to the Entente to return to their former Ally, Russia, Poland, Lithuania, Livonia, Esthonia and Bessarabia. The only thing that was changed was the condition of dependence of the provinces that had been taken away from Russia.

We were also obliged to take up arms again on the Southern half of the Eastern front. True to their principles only to respect the rights of Self-determination when they were to the advantage of the Bolsheviks, the Russian Bolshevik Government had begun warfare against the Ukraine and their governing body—the Rada. The Ukrainian Government was overthrown and driven away.

If the Central Powers, who had made peace with the Ukraine for the sake of bread wanted to get bread, they would have to go and fetch it.

After peace had been signed, the Ukrainian representatives made no secret of the desperate position in which their Government was placed, and quite openly begged assistance from Germany. In my opinion it was a logical necessity for us to accede to this request. Having taken the first step we had to go on ; we had recognized the Ukrainian Government as having the right to exist, and we had concluded a peace with them ; we had therefore to see that the peace we had signed was carried out, and for this purpose the first thing we had to do was to support the Government that had concluded the peace with us.

Therefore our troops marched into the Ukraine. Our advance, chiefly along the railway lines, went rapidly forwards, although we met with opposition in many places. The Bolshevik bands that had been sent to occupy the Ukraine defended themselves, and besides we had many fierce engagements with the Czecho-Slovak Divisions whom we met here for the first time. However, resistance was suppressed everywhere and our troops marched through the whole of the Ukraine as far as the Steppes of the Don.

At first the Austro-Hungarian troops had hesitated to join the advance. The Austro-Hungarian Government wanted peace and the cessation of hostilities and it was with difficulty that they could be persuaded that in the present circumstances a state of peace was impossible, that above all if they wanted to get corn, which was more needed by them even than by Germany, it would be necessary to go and fetch it. We therefore began the advance alone, but the Austrians followed us very soon and then a race for the great object began between us which was often not without friction. While Kiev fell quite without dispute into the German sphere of interest, the Austrians took possession of Odessa and the Odessa railway.

One of the conditions of peace with Soviet Russia naturally concerned the resumption of diplomatic relations. In the meantime I had become sufficiently well acquainted with the Bolsheviks to know the danger there would be in allowing a Bolshevik Embassy to be established in Berlin or consulates to be opened, which would serve as centres for Bolshevik propaganda against Germany. Not for a moment had the Bolsheviks left it in doubt that their object was a World Revolution and that they considered the revolutionizing of Germany was the first step towards it. They used every opportunity for propaganda. Radik, a member of the peace delegation, even went as far as having propaganda writings thrown out of the railway coaches to be distributed among our soldiers. I therefore sent a special warning that a Bolshevik Embassy should not be allowed in Berlin ; I explained my reasons to the General Headquarters and proposed that as long as the state of war lasted the two Ambassadors, both the Russian and the German, should have their residence in the Headquarters of the Commander-in-Chief in the East. Here I would be able to keep in check any too great activity of Mr. Joffé. In any case in this way it would be possible to prevent his having any very close connexion with the German communists. As far as I know the General Headquarters quite agreed with my proposal but it met with opposition from the Foreign Office and came to nothing. His Excellency Kriege, the director of the juridical department of the Foreign Office swore to Joffé's sincerity and was burning with desire to continue in Berlin the negotiations he had begun with him in Brest-Litovsk. Events proved that I had been right in my fears. It was too late when Secretary of State Solf had the case that contained propaganda literature broken open. He locked the stable door after the steed had been stolen.

CHAPTER XVIII

1918

THE military activity of the Commander-in-Chief in the East can be looked upon as concluded at the end of the German advance into the Ukraine, as the little encounters with the Bolshevik bands caused no great trouble. The administrative work was also insufficient to occupy the whole working power of my staff and myself, in consequence of which General Ludendorff took away from the Commander-in-Chief in the East one business after another. Thus General Gröner was sent to Kiev to found a large Germano-Ukrainian business organization there. This organization was brilliant on paper but it produced small results. It will probably never be known if the Ukrainian delegation had over-estimated the existing stock of corn, or whether the peasants hid the remaining stocks of wheat. I think the latter was the case. Whatever may have been the cause our organization was unable to procure any considerable quantities of corn. I think that without having a large central organization we would have been more successful if we had engaged a large number of Jewish dealers and commissioned them to buy the corn for us in the open market. His influence on the political conditions in Kiev was also taken away from the Commander-in-Chief in the East. He had not the slightest influence on the fall of the existing government and the setting up of the Hetmann Skoropadski in its place.

We had the same fate in the Baltic Provinces as we had had in the Ukraine. Here also the Commander-in-Chief in the East was asked in the most amiable form to refrain from interfering, and the 8th Army was commissioned to execute the plans of the General Headquarters for the Baltic Provinces. The new Chief of Staff of this Army, Lieutenant-Colonel Frantz, enjoyed General Ludendorff's special confidence. It is useless to criticise the German policy for the Border States as events drew a thick line through all that Germany had intended to do in the East. I wish only to observe that I personally did not approve of the plan of taking away from Russia all the Baltic Provinces. A great Power like Russia was, and must become again, would in the long run never be able to permit Riga and Reval, which may be called the door keys to its Capital, Petrograd, to be taken away from it. And besides the percentage of the population in Livonia and Esthonia of German origin is not so great as to vindicate the establishment of a purely German rule there.

On the 1st of May, 1918, the Commander-in-Chief in the East removed his Headquarters to Kovno and the Administrative Department returned there too. We had nothing more to do on the Southern half of the front. For the management of internal affairs it was most desirable that the whole staff should be united in one place.

In the meantime until the beginning of March all the troops that were capable of fighting were dispatched from the Eastern front to the West.

For the first time during the whole campaign the West front had superiority in numbers over the adversary. Now General Ludendorff had the difficult decision placed before him, whether he was to use this superiority to make a great and decisive offensive, and if he decided on this move, when and where the attack was to be made. Judging by the experiences that we had had in the West, where the great offensives of the Entente, which had been commenced with enormous numbers of troops and quantities of material, and had been carried out quite regardless of the losses of human life, but still had never ended in a decisive success, some of the German leaders were of the opinion that a German offensive would also fail to attain a great success. It might have been possible to suppose that with a friendly Russia in the rear, from which the starved out Central Powers could obtain provisions and raw materials, they would have decided not to attack in the West, but to await the attack of the Entente. However, these preliminary conditions did not exist at all. The news that came from Russia grew worse every day: atrocities of every description, the massacre of many thousands of the educated and propertied classes, plunder, robbery and such complete disorder that all regular commercial relations were quite out of the question, was what we heard in every report. If it were desired to follow the proposed course of waiting in the West until the Central Powers had received provisions from the East it would be necessary first of all to establish conditions in the East which would produce the necessary preliminary conditions. Every day the Commander-in-Chief in the East received piteous entreaties for help from all classes of the Russian population. The greater number of the reports we received from the delegates we had sent to Russia, asserted it was impossible that we could look on inactive at the atrocities of the Bolshevik rulers—nevertheless everybody must agree that it was a difficult decision for us to make—to denounce the peace that had just been concluded and again recommence hostilities against Russia. I must confess that at first even I was not able to favour such a decision. The weight of the Russian Colossus had pressed politically too heavily on Germany for over a hundred years for a feeling of relief not to be experienced, that the might of Russia had been destroyed for many long years by the Revolution and the Bolsheviks' rule. But the more I heard of the Bolshevik atrocities the more my opinion changed. In my opinion it was impossible, as a respectable man, to stand inactive and allow a whole nation to be butchered. For this reason I got into touch with different representatives of the old Russian Government. Besides a real state of peace did not exist in the East ; we still had a weak, but consecutive line of troops along the front facing the Bolshevik bands ; there was shooting almost every day ; we did not know what was going on in real Russia ; entire obscurity concealed from us the true object ot the Czecho-Slovak legions. As always during war time, the most exaggerated reports of their numbers and their objects reached us ; it was reported that England furnished them with money and that with England's support, they wanted to march from the East on Moscow and take possession of the Government. If that happened Germany would again be surrounded. For these reasons, in the Spring of 1918, I supported the opinion that it would be best to clear the situation in the East, that is, to denounce the peace, to march on Moscow, to form another Russian Government, to grant them better conditions of peace than the Brest-Litovsk Treaty had given them—for instance, at first Poland might be returned to them—and to conclude an alliance with the new Government. The Eastern front would not have required any additional troops for this purpose. Major Schubert, who was our military attaché in Moscow at the time, was the first to support the idea of decisive action against the Bolsheviks, and he considered that two battalions would be sufficient to restore order in Moscow, to overthrow the Bolsheviks and establish a new Government in their place. Although I looked upon his views as somewhat too optimistic, the Divisions that we still had would probably have been sufficient to carry out this plan. At that time Lenin and Trotsky had no Red Army at their disposal. They had their hands fully occupied with disarming the old army and dispatching the soldiers to their homes. Their power was only supported by a few Lettish Battalions and a few hordes of Chinese coolies, who had been armed and were employed, at first, and even now, as executioners.

For instance, we could have advanced on the lines Smolensk-Petrograd, and once arrived there we could have formed a new Government, which would simply have supported the reports that the Tsarevich was still alive and we would have appointed a regent for him. I thought at the time of the Grand Duke Paul with whom, through his son-in-law, Colonel Durnovo, the Commander-in-Chief in the East had been in connexion. The Provisional Government could then have been transferred to

Moscow, where, in my opinion, it would have been a trifle to sweep the Bolshevik Government away. If we had done this Russia would have been spared unspeakable misery and suffering and the lives of millions of her people.   How far such events would have cast their shadow over Germany and the West must be left to the imagination.   It would doubtless have been immense if the German politics and the German High Command had come to this resolve before Ludendorff had made his first offensive in March, 1918.

There can be no doubt that the possibility of establishing orderly conditions in the East, of concluding an alliance with a new Russian Government and of waiting in the West had never entered General Ludendorff's mind.   He was determined to bring about a decision by an attack in the West, and he was convinced that the attack would succeed and that the German Army would conquer.   On the other hand, there were two dangers that had to be taken into consideration, as they might have had to be faced in the West by waiting, and which, as time passed, would certainly become more imminent, these were : the increase of the American troops and the menacing possibility that the adversary would succeed in imitating the new gas.   From the point of view of a military critic nothing can be said against the decision to attack.   It remains to inquire if the execution would also bear criticism, and from this side two points were defective.   The attack was not made solely at the spot that was considered the most favourable for a breach in the line to be made, and it was not made with the whole of the forces that could be disposed of.   The point that was considered as the most favourable was the Southern wing of the English Army to the North of the Somme. All the available forces ought to have been thrown on that one point. Instead of which attacks were made both to the North and the South of the Somme.

In his book that appeared in 1921, entitled, *At the Supreme War Council*, Captain Wright shows us that in spite of this the German attack of March was almost victorious, and we missed winning the War only by a hair's breadth. However, as we did not succeed in taking Amiens and thus separating the English and French Armies—we only almost succeeded, we did not win the victory. Our offensive met with the same fate that the numerous enemy attacks had experienced, it had only indented the enemy front, but it had not broken through it.

The troops that the General Headquarters had at their disposal in the Spring of 1918 were, without doubt, good. It has been proved that both the communists and the socialists had used every expedient to undermine the morale of the troops. By the reports I received from many hundreds of officers whom I questioned on the subject in the Spring of 1918 this agitation had not had any great effect on the troops at the front. In the communication lines the position was worse. The poison that was being spread there penetrated at first but slowly into the troops at the front, and it was only under the influence of the severe fighting during the Summer of 1918 that the decay set in, which brought about the disintegration of the proudest Army that has ever been known in the history of the world.

At the moment when the General Headquarters saw that they would not get Amiens, that they had not been able to break through the enemy's front, they ought to have realized that a decisive victory on the Western front was no longer to be expected. If this first attempt, which had been made with the best forces they possessed, had failed, every succeeding attack that could only be made with ever diminishing forces, would likewise have no chance of success. On the very day on which the General Headquarters gave the order to cease the attack on Amiens, it was their duty to apprise the Government that the time had arrived to proceed to peace negotiations, and that there was no longer any prospect of finishing the War with a decided victory on the Western front.

I do not know if, in April, 1918, it would have been feasible to obtain a reasonable peace, but I think it would have been possible. It would certainly have been a better one than the Peace of Versailles. In any case we ought to have refrained from any further offensives. They only cost us terrible losses—both in men and material which we could no longer replace. Even then it would not have been too late to carry into effect the Russian plan of the Commander-in-Chief in the East. It appears to me doubtful if the nations of the Entente would have had the energy to continue the War if we had established a new Government in Russia in May or June, and concluded an alliance with them. While we remained on the defensive in the West our Government would have offered to make a peace in which the restoration of Belgium would have been guaranteed and perhaps a few districts in Lorraine sacrificed.

The continuation of the offensive required measures that would have been hazardous considering the fighting worth and the morale of the army at the time. The demands on the single Divisions became intolerably great ; the time that they had to remain in the front line without being relieved was too long, good substitutes were not to be found ; the General Headquarters searched for men and scraped them together, wherever they could be found and they were sent to the front to complete the numbers regardless of anything else. Thus all the younger men were taken out of the Eastern Divisions and sent to the West. There was special need of well trained artillery reserves so that all the men who were fairly well fitted for service in the field were taken away from every battery in the East. I am convinced that it was especially this transfer of men from the troops on the Eastern front to the West, that had the most fatal consequences. It was quite evident that the Bolshevik propaganda was working. Although the old discipline held the body of troops together and it was able to count on the whole Army, still it was unfortunately impossible to prevent individuals who were dissatisfied that they had been torn from their units and sent from a quiet front into new fights, from passing on the poison which they had imbibed in the East from Bolshevik theories. In this way decomposing elements were borne to the Western front, which fell upon only too fertile soil in the men who were overtired by continual fierce fighting.

In the same way as General Ludendorff refused to see that the unsuccessful March offensive had definitely deprived the German Army of all prospect of a great victory, so also he closed his eyes to the threatening signs that were visible on the fronts of our Allies. It is true the Turks had still been able to resist the attacks near Jerusalem during April and May and they had retained their

positions there, but the English superiority was
daily making itself more felt. Marshal Liman von
Sanders foresaw the events that inevitably were
bound to occur before the Autumn. He described
the position and asked for help. The German Headquarters paid no attention. Likewise no attention
was paid to the numerous warnings that came from
the Bulgarian front. With the exception of a few
Battalions all the German troops that had formed
the backbone of the Macedonian front had been
taken away for the great battle in the West. A
German victory in the West would have naturally
also saved the Bulgarian front ; as this victory did
not take place they ought, at least, to have thought,
in the Summer of 1918, of sending new German
forces to the Bulgarian front. On the Eastern front
there were troops that they could have disposed of.
For although the Divisions we had on the Eastern
front were chiefly composed of old Landwehr and
Landsturm units and unsuitable to fight on the
Western front, I am convinced that they would
have done their duty on the Bulgarian front.

Thus we drifted into hopeless disaster. Added
to this nobody among the people knew how serious
the situation really was. The announcements of
victory sent out by the General Headquarters after
the March attack, the great honours that were
bestowed on the members of the General Headquarters and the leaders who had taken part in the
attack, caused not only the greater part of the
nation but also the greater part of the Army to
believe that all was going well. We—and also the
Commander-in-Chief in the East—heard nothing
of the heavy losses that the offensive had cost, we
did not know that Germany was no longer in a

position to make good these losses. All in the Army were convinced that the Western front would at any rate be able to hold out. It was only in the Summer that the position became clear to me.

CHAPTER XIX

FINAL REMARKS

BEFORE concluding, I wish to recapitulate once more my opinions on the chances Germany had had in the World War, and the reasons why they were not fully utilized.

In August, 1914, we ought to have won the War in the West in a canter, if Count Schlieffen's original intentions had been carried out ; that is to say, if after breaking through Belgium the right wing had been reinforced and lengthened by all the available forces. That this was not done, but on the contrary that troops were taken from the right wing for the Eastern front was unquestionably a mistake of the first General Headquarters.

But even then the repulse on the Marne ought not to have taken place. That it occurred, that the crisis in which the 2nd Army found itself was not overcome by energetic action, that the decision of the 1st Army to surmount the difficulties by an attack was not supported, but on the contrary, through that unfortunate dispatch of Lieutenant-Colonel Hentsch, with his obscure verbal order and his indecisive authorization, the wonder of the Marne, which the French were unable to understand, was possible, is another omission of the Commander-in-Chief Moltke.

After the repulse on the Marne it was once more

possible to try to make a rush forward, instead of letting the front be strengthened for a trench war. This would have been possible if a decision had been taken to transport at least ten to twelve Army Corps from the left to the right wing and with them to make a grand united attack on that side. That this plan, which was suggested by General Gröner, was not executed is the fault of the second General Headquarters.

As the War was now not to be won in the West, it was necessary to attempt a decision in the East, where events had developed in such a manner that such a decision might be possible. In the late Autumn of 1914 and in the Summer of 1915 two favourable opportunities occurred, that might have led to the complete defeat of the Russian Army. Both these opportunities General Falkenhayn let slip. He is also responsible for the offensive at Verdun, the defective leadership of the Serbian campaign, the failure to take Salonica and the refusal to make a united offensive against Italy. After the opportunity of so completely defeating Russia that she would have been obliged to make peace had not been taken advantage of, it was necessary to clearly understand that according to all human calculations Germany could never win the War.

From that moment all the endeavours of the Government ought to have been directed to the obtaining of a peace with the *status quo ante*, and the exertions of the General Headquarters ought to have been to prevent any repulse from occurring so that the Army might remain in possession of the conquered territories. I believe that such a peace might have been obtained in 1917 if we had quite clearly resigned all claim to Belgium.

Contrary to all expectations, an event occurred at that time which offered the German Empire once again the chance of coming through victoriously out of the War. This was the Russian Revolution which eliminated the numerically strongest opponent and gave us the numerical superiority on the Western front, notwithstanding the enormous numbers of our opponents.

There were two possibilities of profiting by the new position of affairs : either we could decide to put Russia in order, to make an alliance with a new Russian Government, and to bide our time in the West. By this proceeding, it is true, we could not achieve a great victory, but we could never be defeated. Or else to employ the superior numbers we possessed in order to make a great decisive attack. General Ludendorff had decided on the latter possibility. He wanted to conquer, but he had not employed the whole of the forces he possessed nor had he been fortunate in the way he brought them into action. The great attack to break through did not succeed ; instead of realizing then, that the last chance of victory had been forfeited, instead of acting solely on the defensive from that moment, and of letting the Government know that it was high time to try through diplomatic means to attain peace by negotiation, he continued the offensive until the last strength of the Army was exhausted. In this way Ludendorff found himself obliged to ask for an Armistice within twenty-four hours, and he left Germany defenceless to the cold hate of England, the fanatical desire for revenge of France, and a crack-brained Wilson.

Lightning Source UK Ltd.
Milton Keynes UK
UKOW04f1622240118
316764UK00001B/3/P